THE INTERNET MARKETING STRATEGY BOOK

Learn the best methods, and make a realistic plan.

Barry Abraham

© 2013 Barry Abraham
All rights reserved.

http://brickway.net

Table of Contents

Introduction	5
The Parts of This Book	7
Part 1-Get Your Website Right	11
Part 2-Early Stage—Must Dos	25
Part 3- AdWords/Pay-Per-Click	40
Part 4-Search Engine Optimization (SEO)	56
Part 5-The Social Web for Business	72
Part 6-YouTube, Email Marketing, Podcasting, & Craigslist	95
Part 7-Ten Amazing Tools & Timesavers	113
Part 8-Ten Timeless Marketing Principles	134
Part 9-Ten Things Every Entrepreneur Should Know	154
Part 10-Putting Your Plan into Action (Realistically)	175
Appendix	190

To my wife, Karla, and my children, Samuel, Jessica and Sofia.

Thank you for your love and support.

And thanks for understanding while I spent so much time at my computer writing this book.

I love you with all my heart.

XOXO

Introduction

Welcome to *The Internet Marketing Strategy Book*.

If you are in business (or you want to be), your marketing efforts can be a crucial aspect of your business plan. Having a great product or service is a good start, but marketing it can be a make-or-break factor. The Internet has brought big changes to the way businesses approach marketing. The sheer popularity of email, web videos, search engines, social websites, and more makes it a necessity for businesses to leverage these mediums. The risk of ignoring them is too great. Your competitors are jumping onboard—you need to as well.

When I first began learning about Internet marketing, I found it fascinating. I still do. The problem is that (to use a metaphor) you think you are jumping into a swimming pool and then realize you are in the ocean. One minute you are focused on a small facet of Internet marketing, and the next minute you are overwhelmed by how vast the area around you is. You try to progress in one direction, but the winds are blowing you in another, while the current is moving you in yet another. We hear that we need to blog, tweet, use SEO, use AdWords, run email marketing campaigns, make YouTube videos, ask for Facebook "likes," and on and on and on. How are we supposed to do all of these things? How are we even supposed to learn all of these things?

I am writing this book for business owners who need an Internet marketing strategy that is REALISTIC. Let's face it: one could spend weeks, months, or years just studying how to do SEO, AdWords, or some other method in the proper way. I'm guessing you don't have time for that. This book is intended to give you an overview of the most prominent types of Internet marketing and to help you decide which ones are right for your business. In a succinct way, I intend to explain:

- What a particular aspect of Internet marketing is.
- Whether it is right for your business.
- Various ways it could be helpful.
- The most important things to know about it.

- The most important things to do with it.
- The most important things NOT to do with it.

This book tells you what you need to know in order to make a realistic plan—no less, and no more. Time is a precious resource, and I want to help you make the very best use of it. This is the motivation behind both the substance and the style of this book.

Using the Internet for business offers exciting opportunities never before seen in history. It is an endless frontier that anyone with a computer, Internet access, and some ambition can venture into. I hope this book is helpful and enjoyable to you on your quest for online-marketing success.

To contact me, or to see valuable supplements to this book, please go to these links:

www.brickway.net/contact/

www.brickway.net/strategybook/supplements/

I would love to hear any comments from you, and will try to answer any questions that I can.

Side-note fact: What's the difference between advertising and marketing? Advertising is just one component of marketing. Marketing is a much broader subject which can include advertising, public relations, sales strategy, market research, product pricing, and more.

Throughout this book the words *marketing* and *advertising* appear many times. I did my best to use the appropriate term for the subject, but in many instances, either one was applicable. Therefore, my choice of terms could have been random in those instances.

INTRODUCTION

The Parts of This Book

This book is divided into ten sections. Here is a brief summary of each one:

1. **Getting Your Website Right.** This part comes first because a website plays an important role in almost any Internet marketing strategy. Your website is your own piece of virtual real estate that you can customize to be useful for you and your customers. It is the "tip of the spear" to which other marketing efforts play a supporting role. This part explains the importance of your website, the qualities that make a website effective, how to gather the elements you will need, and systems that allow you to create and manage your own website.

2. **Early Stage – Must Dos.** Once you have a website for your business, there are a few things that are important to do right away. These things are important because they don't require a large investment of time, yet they are very beneficial. It is best to get the ball rolling on at least some of these things as soon as possible. Topics covered include Google Analytics, Google Webmaster Tools, registering your business to show up in local search engine listings (if your business is a local one), building citations to help your ranking, blogging and mobile websites.

3. **AdWords/Pay-Per-Click.** In this author's opinion, pay-per-click advertising is the best way to start growing your business immediately. It is a very exciting method with enormous potential for many types of businesses. Its biggest problem, however, is its steep learning curve. Learning to use pay-per-click (PPC) platforms without wasting a lot of money is time consuming. However, whether you want to dive in and try it yourself or find a consultant to help you, this part of the book will give you an overview of the things you need to know. Most of what's covered in this part applies to various PPC platforms, but since Google AdWords is the biggest PPC platform, that is the main topic of this section.

4. **Search Engine Optimization (SEO).** As long as there have been search engines to point us to the information we are seeking, there have been people trying to understand how to make their

web pages appear higher in search engine results. Although the actual formulas (called algorithms) are kept secret, there is a great deal of common knowledge. Some has come from researchers who study the search engines, and some has come from the search engine companies themselves. After all, the search engines want you to succeed legitimately. They don't want you to learn how you might be able to cheat or manipulate their system. This section is meant to inform you of the measures you can take to help your web pages rank higher in natural/organic search results.

5. **The Social Web for Business.** Everybody's doing it, or so it seems. "Like us on Facebook!" "Follow us on Twitter!" These and similar phrases are all around us these days. Is this some kind of weird mania or is it a genuine staple of how marketing should be done today? This section aims to answer that question and many others. It covers the most important aspects of the most prominent social platforms, including Facebook, Twitter, Google+, and LinkedIn.

6. **YouTube, Email Marketing, Podcasting, & Craigslist.** This part covers several big methods that businesses use to stay visible. It's hard to overestimate just how powerful these methods are. YouTube is a free and easy-to-use platform that can have multiple and prodigious benefits for your business. Email marketing is perhaps the best way to stay in the minds of your current customers. It is also fairly easy to do and can be free. Podcasting is an amazingly powerful method for establishing yourself as a knowledgeable authority on a subject. It can be utilized for great marketing benefits. Craigslist is one of the world's most popular websites with over fifty billion page views per month. Using it effectively can be a boon to your business.

7. **Ten Amazing Tools & Timesavers.** As I mentioned in the introduction, Internet marketing is a very big pool in which to swim. It can feel a lot like an ocean. How can you manage to keep your business alive, competitive, and moving forward in the coming years? The answer is: 1. by choosing clear priorities and 2. by using great tools. In this section, I describe some of the best tools for getting your work done efficiently. Software development has come a long way in recent years, and sometimes

Introduction

you need to upgrade to better programs. They help you save time, and that is one of the most important aspects of being successful in business.

8. **Ten Timeless Marketing Principles.** Times change, technology changes, but some things never do. Having a great website, social web marketing system, YouTube channel, AdWords campaign, blog, podcast and email marketing system is mostly a waste without knowing the principles outlined in this section. In the end, it is people who will become your customers. Sure, there are a lot of robots out there vacuuming carpet and performing automatic car washes, but they haven't become actual consumers yet. The more you understand people and how they make their purchasing decisions, the more effective you can make all of your marketing efforts.

9. **Ten Things Every Entrepreneur Should Know.** We live in a big, interconnected world containing approximately seven billion people. Free markets abound, full of amazing products and services—many of which didn't exist a few years ago. Succeeding as an entrepreneur is not easy. It takes focus, persistence and strategic thinking. This section outlines ten principles that all entrepreneurs should understand and keep in the front of their minds as they make decisions and progress toward their goals. Adopting any one of these principles as part of your operational and strategic method could make the difference to bring your dreams of great success to fruition.

10. **Putting Your Plan into Action—Realistically.** The first nine parts of this book are intended to give you the information you need to understand the methods, tools, and principles that can help you succeed in Internet marketing. This last part brings it all together to help you prioritize and make decisions about how to proceed. We all have limited resources. No business has unlimited time and money for marketing. Considering your options carefully, prioritizing your methods wisely, and executing your plan relentlessly is the way for you to move forward. This section will help start you on your way.

Occasionally, I include sidebar items called Side-note facts, Reality checks or Warnings. Side-note facts are little bits of information I wanted to include, but not in the main text. Reality checks are for subjects where there might be a large investment of time involved, and you should think carefully before committing your efforts in that direction. Warnings, of course, point out costly mistakes you will want to avoid.

Part 1-Get Your Website Right

The Importance of Your Website

The Internet was first developed in the 1960s. It was born out of a process known as "internetworking," which allowed separate computer networks to exchange information. The World Wide Web (which is a function of the Internet) was invented in 1990 by Tim Berners Lee. His idea was to have pages that "link" together, creating an efficient means for scientists to share information.

Fast forward a couple of decades. The World Wide Web has grown from a simple means of linking pages to practically a virtual world of its own. It's a major part of everyday life for many people. Facebook, YouTube, Google, and other enormously popular services all grew out of a simple Internet function for linking pages.

If you are a business owner, having a "site" on the web that current and potential customers can access is of great value. It can be a place for educating people about your products or services, a place where they may interact with you, or even a place to make purchases. (Okay, I'm guessing that you know that, and have known that since about 1995, so I'll move on...)

Technology for websites and the web has changed dramatically since 1995. Having a website only scratches the surface of the opportunities available on the web. Now there are also the social web, web videos, search engine optimization, paid ads, etc. This might lead you to ask two questions:

1. Is it still important to have a website?
2. How does a website fit into a larger Internet marketing strategy?

First of all, yes, it is very important to have a website. A website is a piece of virtual real estate that you own and can customize to make it useful for your business. It even has an address that's yours—e.g. http://www.youraddress.com.

Secondly, your website is the home base of your business on the Internet. It's where you want people to go. If they are going to buy from you, leading them here should be a key goal in your marketing strategy. Though you might have a large range of visibility on the Internet (videos, podcasts, tweets, etc.), ideally you want those efforts to drive traffic to your website.

Since your website is your most fundamental presence on the web, it's important for it to be appealing to the people who visit. Step one for your business' online presence is to have a website that is inviting, informative, and representative of the business you own.

Qualities of a Good Website

Let's make one thing clear immediately: people don't care much about your website. They care about what they need or want at the time they visit. Maybe they want to read about your services, maybe they are looking for price information, or maybe they just need your phone number. They only want to find what they're looking for, and have an easy and pleasant time doing it. In other words, they care about your site only insofar as it serves them. Having a super-cool animation on your homepage might be impressive to you. But unless you are in the business of "super-cool" (like a rock star), it probably won't mean much to your visitors. It might be fun to have a cool website, but it's better to have an effective one.

So, what constitutes an effective website for most businesses? First and foremost, a look and a feel. First impressions are important, and most people get a sense of a web page in a fraction of a second. Shapes, colors, layouts, headings, and images tend to give us a feeling. Subconsciously, we do a quick scan that answers some basic questions like: Does this site seem relevant to what I'm looking for? Does this business seem credible and trustworthy? Does this site seem current and fresh, or outdated and stale? Are there indications that other people frequent this site and support this business? How does this site make me feel? Individual elements and the combined effect of those elements give an instinctive or "gut" feeling to the first-time visitor of a website.

Although there are no hard and fast rules about what your website should look like, here are some highly advisable dos and don'ts that you should consider carefully:

DO provide easy navigation

> Most of us have had the experience of visiting a website to look for specific information, only to be frustrated because there's no clear navigation system to guide us. The people who visit your site could be visiting for a variety of reasons. It's important to think of what those reasons might be, and provide a clear path to what they might be looking for. Be sure to have a primary navigation menu that clearly shows where they can go for the information they seek.

DO have a clear CTA (call-to-action).

> Having a clear CTA in a noticeable place on your homepage is highly advisable. You want your visitors to engage with your site and your business somehow. What would you most like them to do? Perhaps you'd like them to watch a video that promotes your products or services. Perhaps you want them to fill out a form to get more information. Or perhaps you'd like them to submit their email address to sign up for your monthly newsletter. Think about how you can get to the next level in your relationships with your website visitors, and encourage an action with a clearly visible CTA.

DO show photos of people's faces.

> One thing that can add warmth and create positive feelings in your website visitors immediately is showing pictures of people's faces. The pictures could be of you. They could be of your employees. Or they could be of a happy family that uses (or appears to use) your products or services. Studies have shown that people pay more attention to ads and web pages showing human faces. (Warning: Be sure to have the permission of the people in the photos before using them on your web pages. And be sure you have the legal rights to use any photographs that appear on your website. See more about finding photos in the "Gathering Elements for Your Website" section below.)

DON'T have a cluttered look.

> Keep the overall layout in mind as you add elements to your web pages. Adding too many elements to a page can look cluttered, unorganized, and unprofessional. It can also distract from the primary messages you want to convey to visitors, such as your CTA.

DON'T have web pages that are too slow to load.

> Customers (and therefore new business) can be lost due to slow-loading web pages. You want to keep that from happening as much as possible. One thing to always remember is that the speed at which web pages load depends on how fast the visitor's Internet connection is. Although a page might load fast for you, it might not for someone else. There is a tradeoff that comes with having large image or animation files as part of your web pages. For most businesses, it's better to err on the side of "fast" rather than "fancy."

> For a list of ways to keep your website loading fast, and some great tools for speed-testing, visit www.brickway.net/strategybook/page-load-speed/.

DO keep consistent color and style elements on all pages of your site.

> People like consistency. Certain colors, layout styles, menus and other visual elements create a certain look and feel. Keeping these elements as consistent as possible on all of your pages is much better than a hodgepodge that seems thrown together quickly and cheaply.

DON'T have misspellings and bad grammar in your text.

> Few things are a bigger turn-off than having misspellings and bad grammar on your website. Your website represents your business. Potential customers like to see businesses that are professional, credible and trustworthy. If it appears that you don't pay attention to the details of your website, they might think that you don't manage your business well. Take the time to properly check your spelling and grammar.

DON'T make the site all about you.

> Try to make your site as much about your visitors as possible, and less about you and your business. It's easy to fall into the trap of simply touting the accomplishments of the business, rather than emphasizing how the business can serve the website visitor. In other words, instead of the message being "Here's why we are so great and wonderful," the message should be "Here's how we can make your life easier and better." Be sure to emphasize the benefits potential customers can get from your products or services.

DO have an "About" page

> It's true that your website should emphasize the benefits your products or services can provide for your visitors, but sometimes visitors really want to know who you are. Because of this, you should give them this information in the form of an "About" page. The page can be called "About Us" or something similar, but the name should indicate that it's the place to go to find more information about you. An effective "About" page is one that reveals authentic details about the business and the people who run it. Using stories and images can be helpful. Visitors to your site should get the feeling they have seen a real person or real people from reading your "About" page.

DO have a blog

> Although it requires a steady investment of time, blogging is one of the best investments you can make for your website, as well as your online marketing strategy as a whole. Blogs keep websites fresh and add content that can keep visitors on your site longer. They can help with SEO (search engine optimization) in several ways, and they can complement any social media strategy very nicely. Websites with blogs get much more traffic than websites without them. One of the great things about blogs is that there are really no rules for them. They can be as simple or elaborate as you want them to be. (*For more about blogging, see Part 2 of this book.*)

Gathering Elements for Your Website

Web pages and websites are usually combinations of different elements. Although you could simply have a one-page website with nothing more than some text in the middle, that probably wouldn't be very effective for your business. Much of the work of web design is in finding and creating the different elements that will make up your site. Putting the elements together into a site might be something you want to do yourself, or you might want to hire someone else to do it for you. Either way, though, it will be much easier and faster (and less expensive, if you are paying someone) to have as many of the different elements as possible prepared in advance.

The following is a list of elements you might want to work on and gather before putting your site together.

- Web hosting account – Although this is not an element of your website per se, it is an important aspect of what you will need. Websites and the data they are comprised of reside on computers called "servers." The job of a server is simply to "serve" information that is requested. For example, when someone clicks on a link to one of your web pages, they are essentially requesting that page's information from the server. It's a bit like ordering something at a restaurant: you order something from the menu, and a server delivers what you order. To be able to serve up web pages quickly and efficiently, there are services called "web hosts" that provide and manage servers. You will need an account with a web host that will house your website on its servers. (I highly recommend Bluehost as a web host. To learn more about Bluehost, go to www.brickway.net/bluehost/.)

- Domain name – Your domain name is the unique name your website will have on the web. For example, in "http://www.brickway.net" the "brickway.net" part is the domain name. There is an international registry of domain names. You will need to find one that suits your business and is available, and then register it. There are many services that do this, but again I recommend Bluehost. (To learn more about registering a domain name on Bluehost, go to www.brickway.net/bluehost-domain-names/.)

- Logo – Do you have a logo for your business? Are you planning on getting one? Having a logo can be a nice design element on a website. A good logo adds style and can help make visitors feel that your business is well-established, organized and credible.

- Images – These are very important. As I mentioned earlier, having images of people's faces can make a web page look warmer, friendlier and more appealing. You might want to have other types of pictures as well, however, especially ones that show the products or services your business provides. Having good images prepared and ready helps when it's time to put your site together. If you don't already have some good images to use, you are in luck. There are several large photo downloading services that grant you the right to use their pictures in exchange for a fee. The fees are usually reasonable, and the photos are often amazing. You can search to find almost any kind of image you want. (For a list of some good photo downloading sites, go to www.brickway.net/photo-downloading-sites/). Warning: do not use any images on your website that you don't have the legal right to use.

- Authority badges – Do you belong to any organizations related to your field? Many professional organizations have a graphic you can use on your website if you are qualified and have permission.

- List of web pages – How many pages would you like your website to have and what should they be about? Having this planned is very helpful before getting to work on your site.

- Text – One of the biggest elements to tackle is having the text written for your web pages. This can be difficult and requires some writing skill. Most business websites have some text on every page to explain one thing or another. Many of the visitors to your site won't read much of the text. Most people tend to look at the images, read the headings, and then barely glance at the actual blocks of text. However, it's important to have it there anyway. The whole idea of your website is that visitors can easily find what they want. It's best to give them a variety of ways to get their information. Text is also an important aspect of SEO (search engine optimization). Search engine spiders notice the words used in the text to help index web pages correctly.

- CTA ("call-to-action") – Have you decided on a CTA? Give some thought to what action you would like your website visitors to take, such as calling for an estimate, opting-in for your email newsletter, or filling out a request form.

- Email Opt-In – If you are planning on doing email marketing, you will probably want to have an email opt-in field on your homepage somewhere. This simply says "Hey, if you want to be on my email list, submit your email address here." If you mention that their email address will not be sold or given away to anyone, and give them a good incentive to submit them (such as a free gift), you will often get visitors to opt in. (See more about email marketing in Part 6 of this book.)

- Contact form – Would you like to have a form for visitors to fill out in order to contact you, make comments or request information? If so, what fields would you like the form to have?

- List of products or services – Would you like to have a special page with a list of products or services you provide? Preparing this list is good preparation for building your site.

- Embedded videos – Are there certain sections of your site you would like to have videos in? Creating the videos in advance is a good idea in preparing to build your website.

Need-To-Know Stuff About Web Page Technology

Web design can be a bit complicated. Unfortunately, it's not like designing a poster or a brochure. In fact, you have only limited control of how your finished design will look to a visitor to your site. There are several reasons for this, but here are a few of the key ones:

- People will be looking at your site on different-sized monitors, tablets, and even on smartphones.

- Web pages are viewed through programs called "browsers" (Internet Explorer, Safari, Firefox, Google Chrome, etc.) which are programmed to display various elements differently. Each browser shows its own interpretation of how a web page should look. Browsers must act like translators that take the code and turn it into a graphic display. There are differences in the way different browsers do this.

- Users often customize their browser settings to change the way pages and page items are displayed. For example, they might set their browsers to not show images in an effort to speed up the load time. Or they might set their browsers to show the text larger than usual if they have problems with their vision.

The web has added enormous amounts of new functionality over the years, and this means that web pages are made up of many sophisticated kinds of programming code. Although there are some geniuses out there who can still hand-code sophisticated web pages, most of the web design world now relies on platforms that do most or all of the code work for them.

Wouldn't it be great if there were a way to have a solid, attractive and consistent website structure; to be able to customize the various design aspects; and then to be able to input your own content to fill up the empty spaces? Enter the world of the CMS!

What is a CMS?

A CMS, or content management system, is a software system that lets you create and control a website through a simple interface. This is a perfect solution for those of us who want to be able to manage our own websites without having to learn programming code. CMS systems have risen to enormous popularity, and have grown to include an incredible amount of functionality. If there is a certain function or feature you want your website to have, chances are there is a way to do it through a good CMS.

CMS systems have a "front-end" and a "back-end." Imagine a beautiful toy store. It's nicely arranged and decorated, but the shelves are empty. In the back room (back-end) there is a system of organization for all of the items that will go on the shelves. From the back room, items can be created, gathered, stored, and then made visible in the front-end when the time is right. This is basically how a CMS works. You choose a layout and style for the front-end, and then use the back-end to arrange content in the empty spaces provided by the front-end.

The three most popular CMS platforms are WordPress, Joomla and Drupal. All three are free to use and have a wide range of capabilities. On these platforms, your content is organized in a database and is called up (or requested) by PHP programming in various spaces on your pages. Each has a back-end interface for the non-technical among us that can be used without the need for programming. All three are developed and maintained by a community of thousands of people. They are all "open-source" systems, meaning that people who want to develop additional capabilities such as add-ons, plug-ins and extensions are able to do so. Here is a very brief description of each:

WordPress (www.WordPress.org)

> WordPress is the most popular CMS by far. It started out as a system for blogging but has developed into a robust web design platform. It is widely known to be the most user-friendly of the three largest CMS platforms.

Joomla (www.joomla.org)

> The second most popular CMS platform is Joomla. Although not quite as easy to use as WordPress, Joomla is still fairly simple and user-friendly. It has a wide range of capabilities and some consider it to be more solid and stable than WordPress for certain functions.

Drupal (www.drupal.org)

> Drupal is the third most popular CMS and the most technically demanding. Although it can be used without any programming, it is geared more toward web programmers and developers. It is considered by some to be better than WordPress or Joomla for handling larger and more advanced websites.

My CMS platform of choice? WordPress. I like WordPress for the following reasons:

- It is easy to install, learn, and use.

- It has different administration levels and accessibility options which are helpful for collaboration.

- There are loads of plug-ins available to add functionality and ease to different processes.

- It is very SEO-friendly, meaning it has features to help you optimize your pages so they will be noticed and ranked by the search engines (learn more about SEO in Part 4 of this book).

- There are loads of themes available. (Themes are chosen in WordPress to give websites their style and structural elements. Many are free, but some require a fee to use.)

Starting With WordPress

If you are planning on creating and managing your own website, I highly recommend using WordPress. For the reasons mentioned above, WordPress is a great platform to work with. It's not, however, something you can master in a few minutes or hours. It takes a bit of time and practice. The good thing is that there are many resources out there to help you learn. You can find great articles, forums, and tutorials to make learning much easier. A good place to start is www.WordPress.org.

> *Reality check*: Do you want to learn WordPress? Do you have time to learn WordPress? Perhaps the answers are "no" and "no." So, how can you control your own website content, have it displayed nicely, and keep your costs down without having to completely master WordPress? By getting help. As I mentioned, WordPress is an extremely popular platform. There are scores of people out there who can assist you in getting your site going and keeping it going. Feel free to contact me if you'd like (www.brickway.net/contact/) and I will help you get going. It's also easy to find experts on Elance.com who will help you for a reasonable price. To be clear, this is what I'm suggesting:
>
> 1. Get your hosting account set up (see above).
> 2. Register your domain name (see above).
> 3. Find someone to help you install WordPress, install a theme, and get a few pages started.

> 4. Spend a few hours learning WordPress basics so you won't need help to make simple changes or additions to your site.
>
> This is what I recommend for most people to begin creating and managing their websites. It doesn't take much time or money, and it allows you to be in control.

Whether you decide to go it alone on WordPress or get some help, you will need to learn some fundamental facts about how it works. Here are a few:

- WordPress is software that runs on a web server, not on your own computer. To use it, you need to have a web host and an Internet connection.

- Most major web hosting companies have a very easy method of installing the WordPress software for your site. It often requires just a few clicks.

- Once WordPress is installed and associated with your domain name, you login to the Dashboard, which is the back-end of your website. To login, you simply go to *http://www.yourwebsiteaddress.com/wp-admin* and then enter your username and password (which were established when you installed WordPress).

- The most significant decision for your new site is deciding on a WordPress theme. Themes are collections of templates that determine the layout, look, and style of your pages. There are tens of thousands of themes available (if not more). Some are free, some are available for purchase. WordPress comes with a default theme preloaded, so you have the option of simply using the default theme. To look for more themes, go to the dashboard in WordPress, then click on *Appearance*, then *Themes*. You will see an option to search for available themes.

The theme I prefer to use is called the SmallBiz theme. I find it to have a nice appearance, great functionality, and an extremely easy-to-use set-up panel. It also has technical support for any problems you might have while using it to build your site. For more information about the SmallBiz theme, go to www.brickway.net/smallbiztheme/.

Other places to look for WordPress themes:

    www.themeforest.com
    www.eleganthemes.com
    www.ithemes.com

Summary

Most important things to know from this section:
- Your website is the "home base" of your Internet marketing efforts. Make sure it represents your business well.
- Your website should be uncluttered, easy to read, and easy to navigate.
- Your website should have a clear call-to-action and easy-to-find contact information.
- Your website should have content that interests your visitors and keeps them from going away too quickly – videos, bulleted lists, articles, etc.
- Using a CMS (content management system) is a way to create and manage a website through a user-friendly interface.
- WordPress is a great, free, and immensely popular CMS.
- Having a blog is one of the most important parts of an effective Internet marketing strategy. There are multiple benefits to having a blog. (Learn more about blogging in Part 2 of this book.)

Most important things to do:
- Create an attractive and user-friendly website.
- Use images that show human faces to make your site feel warm and welcoming.
- Have a clear CTA (call-to-action) on your website.

- Use a CMS (content management system) such as WordPress so that you can easily control and manage the site. Perhaps hire a consultant to assist and mentor you along the way.
- Have a blog and post regularly.

Most important things NOT to do:
- Have a cold, unfriendly site. There is a great saying: "People buy from people, not from websites." Humanize your site by having photos of yourself or other people. Have an "About" page with some sincere information about you and the people in your business.
- Forget to have a strong and clear CTA (call-to-action)
- Have pages that are too cluttered, or too slow to load.
- Make the site all about your business rather than addressing your visitors' needs.
- Pay too much for web design services. If you hire someone to design your site, make sure they are using a CMS so that you can log in and be able to make some changes and additions yourself.

Part 2—Early Stage—Must Dos

Part 1 dealt with setting up a website that is effective and manageable. Part 2 is about taking the next steps toward a more complete Internet marketing strategy. The things I mention in this part are important, and the earlier you do them the better. They have to do with checking the overall health of your website, getting data about the number of people visiting your website, the actions visitors are taking (or not taking) while at your site, blogging, getting listed as a local business (if you are a local business) by the search engines for their local results, and building citations (mentions of your business information) on various sites around the web.

Google Webmaster Tools

You want to have web pages that show up in Google searches, right? Well, Google wants to help you. They want to give you hints, ideas, and information to help you succeed in your high-ranking efforts. In fact, they offer a free set of tools to help you do just that. Google Webmaster Tools is the place to go to learn about the relationship between your website and Google's search engine. Although Google won't tell you exactly what to do to be ranked number one, you will find a lot of information that will help you on your way.

Access to Google Webmaster Tools is free, and the set-up process is fairly painless. Once you've set up an account and added your website (you can actually add up to 1,000 websites to one account), you can get information that will help guide your efforts to rank better with Google. One of the great things about using GWT, and one of the reasons that I'm strongly recommending it, is that it doesn't need to take up much of your time. An occasional look to see what's happening will give you valuable insight you wouldn't have otherwise.

How to get started with Google Webmaster Tools?

To start using Google Webmaster Tools, go to www.google.com/webmasters/tools/ and create an account, or sign in using an existing Google account. The next step is to add your site by clicking the "Add a

Site" button. Adding a site to your GWT account involves a verification process. Google wants to make sure you own the site before you may start tracking data from it. You will see several options for site verification, so pick the one that is easiest for you. Once your site has been verified, you will then be able to start viewing data about how your site is being seen and found on Google.

Features of Google Webmaster Tools

Google Webmaster Tools has a wide array of features and can give you valuable information about many aspects of your site's performance. As time goes on, Google adds even more features to give you more information. Here are some of the key things you can do while looking at the data in GWT:

- View the dashboard. Here you can get a quick view of the most relevant information about your site, as well as messages that might come from Google. The "Site Messages" area of the dashboard is where Google sends messages about any problems it might have encountered while crawling on your site.

- View crawl data. Here you can see the data Google has gathered by examining your site, such as errors that might have occurred, the number of times your site has been crawled, and whether the Googlebot found any malware there.

- View traffic data. Traffic data is information about the people who visit your site, and the way they arrived there. Did they search Google to find your page? What words did they search for? Or, did they get to your page through a link on another web page somewhere?

- View optimization data. Viewing the optimization data helps you improve your pages to be better understood by Google, which will hopefully lead to higher rankings in the search results. Here you can see what keywords the Googlebot found to be most prominent on your pages, which can be instructive for making changes.

- If you add or make changes to your web pages, you can ask Google to crawl it sooner to note the changes. This is called the "Fetch as Google" feature.

- View and download data regarding external and internal links to your web pages.

- The "Search Queries" page gives valuable data such as which queries people made that resulted in your web pages being displayed in the search results, the number of times your web pages appeared in the search results (known as "impressions"), the number of clicks that were made on your links in the search results, the CTR (click-through-rate) of your links in the search results, and the average ranking of your links in the search results.

- Use the Change of Address tool to tell Google if your website has moved to a different domain address.

> *Side-note fact*: Bing also has a webmaster tools service, which can be found at www.bing.com/toolbox/webmaster/.

Google Analytics

So you have a website. Perhaps you have other Internet marketing methods working for your business as well, such as a blog, a Facebook page, YouTube videos, or Google AdWords ads. This could be an effective set of marketing initiatives. Question: what would make this set of initiatives even better? Answer: information. Imagine being able to "keep score" and examine which of your marketing efforts are paying off and which aren't. Having a way to track results is invaluable. After all, why keep doing something if it isn't getting the desired results? And why not double-up on the things that are working well? The best way to get results for your marketing efforts is to use an analytics platform, such as Google Analytics.

Google Analytics is a free service intended to give you important information related to your website. It tells you how many visitors you receive, where those visitors were referred from (such as your Facebook page, a particular blog post, or an AdWords ad), how much time visitors spend on your page, and a host of other information. Google Analytics is such a large and robust platform that it can deliver data that is segmented, filtered, and customized only for the things you want to know about your website visitors. If you have an ecommerce website, using Google Analytics can be the linchpin for making your business a success. The information you get from Analytics is like the information an airline pilot gets when he looks at his gauges. That information tells the pilot the direction he is going in, and other key information he needs to decide whether he is on course. If he makes a change, the gauges show him the various results and ramifications that came from that change. In the same way, Google Analytics gives you the key data you need to guide the direction of your marketing efforts and shows you the results and ramifications that come from new moves and changes.

The field of analytics has become very sophisticated in recent years. Website analytics is an industry all its own, with researchers and experts constantly finding ways to learn more about the people who visit certain websites and the actions they take while there. Professional marketers always need to be testing new designs, new slogans, new logos, new promotions, etc. If there is one thing that marketing researchers have learned well, it's that small (even tiny) changes to seemingly insignificant parts of an ad can significantly alter the response of potential customers. The field of analytics lets marketers test different elements of web pages to find out which perform better.

Should you use Google Analytics for your business?

If you have a website for business, then yes, you should use Google Analytics. Even if you have a very small business without much website traffic, you should still use it. Why, you ask? Because it's free, it's not that difficult to set up, and it will definitely give you useful information. Although there can be a learning curve for some of the terminology and concepts involved, it is still fairly simple to take a glance and understand the basics. It's kind of a "no-lose" proposition.

Features of Google Analytics

- Learn how many visitors you get on each page of your site.
- Learn how much time your visitors spend on your pages.
- Learn the "bounce rate," or the rate at which people quickly leave your page without spending more than a few seconds on it.

Early Stage—Must Dos

- Link with Google AdWords for data to help guide your AdWords campaigns.

- View extensive reporting of traffic sources. Find out which of your advertising methods is generating the most visitors to your website.

- Learn about the devices people are using to view your web pages.

- Define "goals" and learn the rate at which you are succeeding with your visitors. Various types of goals can be set, including the visitor viewing a particular page on your site, viewing a video, submitting their email address, spending a specified amount of time on your site, or viewing a specified number of pages.

- Link your Analytics account to Google Webmaster Tools.

- Track the success of your email marketing campaigns by knowing how many of the emails lead to a visit to your website, and possibly some action after that – such as a purchase or other goal.

- Learn which of your web pages is the most frequently visited.

- Apply "remarketing" techniques, which means setting up special ads that will only be displayed to people who have already visited your website.

- Learn which keywords bring the most traffic to your website.

- Set up reports to be sent to you automatically by email on a scheduled basis that you choose.

As I mentioned above, Google Analytics is very robust. This list of features only scratches the surface of what it can do. Simply put, if you have a website for business, you should use Google Analytics. Also, the more time and money you invest into Internet marketing, the more you should integrate the various features of Analytics to help you measure the success of your investments. Tracking the results of specific efforts is a key part of marketing success. Don't fly blind.

How is Google Analytics different from Google Webmaster Tools?

Although there is some overlap in the services provided by Google Analytics and Google Webmaster Tools, there are significant differences in the two services. Google Webmaster Tools is primarily meant to inform you about data that relates to the relationship between your site, the Googlebot, and the Google search engine. Analytics is meant to give you a much wider range of data that can show various types of activity on your website, where that activity and traffic originates from, and more. It is best to sign up for both (remember, they are free) and then link the accounts together.

Here is a summary of each service to give you an overview of the differences:

Google Analytics tells you: The number of visitors, the number of new visitors compared to returning visitors, which pages are most popular with your visitors, data related to your specified goals, extensive information about the sources of your website traffic, information about the devices people are using to view your pages, and more.

Google Webmaster Tools tells you: Crawling errors that may have occurred when the Googlebot attempted to crawl your site, information about search queries that lead to your pages being displayed in Google search results, information about malware that might appear on your site, HTML errors on your site, and more.

How do you start using Google Analytics?

Google Analytics functions from a JavaScript tracking code that is put into the source code of your web pages. This code is not visible to visitors of your website. It only gets noticed by the computers that serve and load your web pages. Through this tracking code, Google Analytics is able to monitor the activity on your website.

To start using Google Analytics for your website, follow these steps:

- Go to www.google.com/analytics/ and sign up for an account.

- Set up account properties.

- Set up the tracking code. During the setup process, GA will give you the tracking code you will need to attach to your web pages. Within the source code of your web pages, the tracking code should be placed just before the </head> tag.*

Google Analytics will then begin tracking activity on every web page on your site that has the tracking code installed.

* If you are using WordPress for your website, find out how to install the Google Analytics tracking code at www.brickway.net/install-analytics-tracking-code-in-WordPress/.

Blogging

The word blog is a contraction of the words "web log." A blog is simply a place to post information about something on the web. For example, if someone is searching for the perfect cheesecake recipe and wants to keep their friends and family updated on the project, they might have a blog for that. The posts can consist of a few lines of text, a picture, a video, a voice recording, or a mixture of these things. There are no rules governing what blogs should be about, or what the blog posts should consist of. If you wanted to have a blog called "Alphabet Letters of the Day" and post one letter of the alphabet every day that would count as a blog. The beauty of blogs is that they can be whatever you want them to be.

Should you have a blog for your business?

If you are serious about using the Internet to grow your business (as you should be), the answer is yes. Here are a few reasons why you should have a blog:

- Websites with blogs get much more traffic than websites without blogs.

- Blogs help make your website "sticky," meaning people spend more time on it. This helps convert people into customers and can help your search engine rankings as well.

- Blog posts give you an opportunity to use keywords that can act as magnets for drawing traffic to your website.

- Websites that get updated with content regularly are more likely to rank higher in search results.

- The content you use in your blog posts gives you something to promote on social websites like Twitter and Facebook.

- If your blog is hosted on your own website, that means you own it. No matter how many Facebook "likes" your business may have, you don't own it. Facebook always has the ability to shut you down for whatever reason. Not only does ownership give you control of your destiny, it also allows you to make an income if your blog starts attracting a large audience (through affiliate marketing or Google's AdSense program).

The best advice I have for you about blogging is just to do it, and to do it systematically. Don't be over-ambitious and try to write a 400-word article every few days. Start simple with a routine you can stick with for the long haul. Maybe it's a 60-word post every week, or maybe it's a photo with a caption every week. Incorporate keywords that are relevant to your products or services. This will help you get traffic from the search engines.

If you really don't want to blog or think you won't have the time to do it regularly, consider having someone do it for you. Do you have a friend or family member who might like to help? It's always possible to hire someone too. Elance.com is a great place to find freelancers with many types of specialties, including blogging for businesses. You can also contact me at www.brickway.net/contact/.

Citations

I know what you're thinking: "Citations… what the heck are those?" Well, it's good to know what citations are because they are an important part of a good Internet marketing strategy—especially for businesses that operate locally. In a nutshell, citations are simple mentions of your business on web pages around the web. They can be on your accountant's website. They can be on your friend's cat's website. They can even be on your own website! That's right, if you put your business name, address and phone number on your own website it counts as a citation.

The main reason citations are important is that they help your business rank better on search engine results pages—especially in the local results section. When you think about this, it makes sense. Like most businesses, search engines strive to do a good job serving their customers. This means they want to give quality results when people search. Since the search engines want to give quality results, they look for aspects of credibility from the websites they index. When they see consistent information about a business in various places around the web, the business appears more credible. On the other hand, if the search engine indexes a website that seems to have no citations/mentions of it anywhere on the web, the business appears less credible. A business can also appear less credible if the search engine finds inconsistent information about it.

The NAP is most important

As I mentioned above, it is bad if the search engines find inconsistent information about a business around the web. Search engines like to see consistency, especially with key information about a business. The most important information to keep consistent is the name, address, and phone number of a business (thus the acronym NAP). Always be watchful and careful that the NAP of your business appears consistently whenever it appears on the web. If you find there are inconsistencies, take measures immediately to try to correct them. One thing to be wary of in particular is call tracking. Call tracking is a commonly used technique to test the effectiveness of an advertisement. A unique phone number is displayed so that any calls that come to that number can be attributed to the ad it came from. If you are using or might someday use call tracking, be sure to keep the call tracking phone number away from any web pages that could be indexed by the search engines and therefore create an inconsistent citation.

Your most important citations

Citations do not all hold equal weight. Having a citation on your friend's cat's website is not as valuable as having a citation on a large directory site like Yellowbook. In fact, establishing citations on large directory sites is something you should do as early as possible. Many large directory sites allow you to list your business for free. Some have a verification process to prove that the information you enter is correct, but many do not. How many citations should you have? There is no magic number, but if I were you I would want to have at least a few more than my closest competitor. Frankly, the more the better.

How to build effective citations

As previously mentioned, having a consistent name, address, and phone number is the most important thing to keep in mind when building citations. Here are a few other tips:

- Fill in as much information as you can on directory sites. Many of them give you the opportunity to put photos, videos, hours of operation, descriptions of your business, a link to your website, links to your social web pages, and more. Not only does a more complete citation look better to a search engine, but it can also help bring traffic to your website directly.

- Make sure you categorize your business correctly and use good keywords to describe what your business does.

- You will need to create usernames and passwords for each directory site, so have a good way of organizing them as you go. Using a spreadsheet is a good method of doing this.

- Use software like LastPass or Roboform to speed up the process of typing the same information into the form fields of the directory sites.

- Remember that any web page that shows a mention of your business is a citation. This can be your Facebook page, your Google+ page, or even your own website.

- Keep an open mind about where on the web you can build citations. Be sure to search the names of your competitors to see where their citations reside on the web.

Some websites where you can build citations for your business

Here are some directory websites where you can register your business and create a citation. Be sure to supply as much information as possible, including photos.

> www.dexknows.com
> www.yellowbook.com
> www.merchantcircle.com
> www.yelp.com
> www.yellowpages.com
> www.supermedia.com
> www.manta.com
> www.local.com
> www.citysearch.com
> www.patch.com

To see a more extensive list, go to www.brickway.net/building-citations/.

Register Your Local Business

One of the major waves that has brought changes to search engines in recent years is an emphasis on local business—and for good reason. If someone searches "pizza restaurant" while in Hazelton, Pennsylvania, they don't want to see results showing pizza restaurants scattered across the United States or in other countries. Most likely they are searching for a pizza restaurant in or around Hazelton, Pennsylvania. Delivering search results with an emphasis on local businesses was a challenge for the search engines. It required a whole new approach for indexing and ranking websites. For the past several years, the search engine companies have developed and refined their approaches and are now quite adept at delivering the local results searchers are looking for.

If you are a local business owner, it is important to be seen in local results. The first step toward doing this is to register your business directly with the search engines. This is a simple process, but requires a verification step to make sure your business exists where you say it does. Go to the following web pages to get started with registering your business on Google, Yahoo, and Bing:

www.google.com/+/business/
www.listings.local.yahoo.com/
www.bingplaces.com/

After you register

After you've registered and verified your business with the search engines, there is more work to do. Ranking higher on the results pages is very beneficial. Often, measures need to be taken to make your listing rise to the top of the list. Keep in mind that people will be able to leave reviews of your business on these sites. Customer interaction tends to benefit your rankings, but negative reviews can damage your reputation. Some things you will want to do are: monitor any reviews that come in, alter your listing information to keep it current, and take measures that can lead to higher rankings.

How to rank higher in the local search results

As I mention in Part 4 of this book (on search engine optimization), search engines keep their formulas for ranking top-secret. They do, however, divulge certain information. With the help of researchers and web professionals, much can be gleaned by simply performing tests to see what seems to work and what doesn't. Here is a list of factors commonly believed to positively influence rankings in local search results:

- The distance from the city centroid (a shorter distance from the city centroid can be a positive ranking factor)
- Number and quality of citations
- Number, quality, and diversity of reviews
- Number and quality of links to your website (known as "backlinks")

Mobile Website

What is a mobile website? A mobile website is a version of your website that is easier to see and navigate on a smartphone, such as an iPhone. Web servers can tell which type of device is requesting web pages. If your site has a mobile version, it will serve that version to any smartphone that requests your website.

What's good about a mobile site? A mobile site condenses the most important features of your site so that a visitor can access the information they desire more easily. Large buttons that say "Directions" "Hours of Operation" or "Call Now" are useful for mobile websites. The "Call Now" button will initiate a phone call on the smartphone.

Having a mobile website is highly recommended, especially for local businesses. People are using their home computers less and less and their smartphones more and more these days. Fortunately, it's not too complicated to have a mobile website. There are services available that make it simple and inexpensive. For more information go to www.brickway.net/mobile-website-service/.

Summary

Most important things to know from this section:
- Blogging is one of the most beneficial things you can do as part of an Internet marketing strategy. It brings more traffic to your website, keeps your website looking current and fresh, and gives you content to promote on social sites like Twitter and Facebook.
- Signing up for Google Webmaster Tools is free and useful. It doesn't require much time to look at occasionally. It is a good service that anyone who cares about Google search ranking and traffic should take advantage of.
- Using Google Analytics is important because it gives a wide range of information about your website's visitor activity. It can tell you which of your online efforts are bringing in the most traffic. For example, you can learn whether your Facebook page gets you more traffic than your YouTube videos. It allows you to define goals and tells you the results of how successful you are in reaching them. Not using Google Analytics (or another similar platform) is like flying blind with your marketing efforts. You won't have a good way of gauging the value of different approaches to your Internet marketing.
- "Citations" are mentions of your business on any page around the web. They are valuable because they can lead to direct traffic to your website and can also lead to higher rankings on search engine

results pages. Adding your business to online directories (such as Yellowbook and SuperMedia) results in valuable citations. The more citations you have, the better—but they must be consistent. Mostly, they must be consistent with the NAP (name, address, and phone number).

- The search engines have become adept at giving local results for people searching for local businesses. Showing up in these listings is very valuable. The first thing businesses need to do to appear in these listings is register with the search engines.

- Mobile websites can help potential customers connect with your business more easily. For example, if someone is out shopping and decides they want to find a particular item at a bakery, they can search Google, find a bakery in the local results, look at the mobile website of the bakery, and then press the "Call" button to be connected immediately to find out whether the desired item is available.

Most important things to do:

- Sign up for your free Google Webmaster Tools account, add and verify your site, and then check your account occasionally to learn about how Google interacts with your site.

- Sign up for your free Google Analytics account, then paste the JavaScript tracking code you receive in the <head> section of your web pages (this is found in the html code of the web pages). Once this is done, you can begin to see valuable information about the visitors to your web pages.

- Start a blog and commit to adding something to it on a regular basis. There is no right or wrong schedule for posting. Each time you post quality information on your blog it has the potential to draw new visitors to your site and new customers to your business.

- Start building citations for your business. You want a consistent name, address and phone number for your business to appear on various places around the web. A good place to start is with large directory sites, such as Yellowbook and SuperMedia. (For a large list of sites to build citations on, visit www.brickway.net/building-citations/.)

Early Stage—Must Dos

- Consider having a mobile version of your website. A mobile site means having a version of your site that is condensed and easier to navigate if someone is looking on their smartphone. It can have ease-of-use features as well, such as a "Call Now" button that will initiate a phone call.

- Register your local business with the search engines. This is a free and simple process that has the potential to give great visibility to your business. Don't wait on this. Do it as soon as possible.

Most important things NOT to do:

- Ignore the free services of Google Webmaster Tools and Google Analytics.

- Delay building citations for your business on large directory sites.

- Have inconsistent NAP (name, address, phone number) information around the web for your business.

- Delay registering your local business with the search engines.

- Miss the opportunity of having a mobile website for visitors using smartphones.

Part 3- AdWords/Pay-Per-Click

Magazines have advertisements. Radio has advertisements. TV and newspapers have advertisements. Why shouldn't web pages? Many of them do, of course. The problem is that there are billions of web pages on the web. How can advertising be sold in a market that is so spread out, so diverse, and so enormous? What kind of system can accommodate the needs of the advertisers themselves so that they have control over the costs, appearances and placements of their ads? Well, a computer system, of course—a very clever and amazing one.

Enter the world of PPC (pay-per-click). With PPC, advertisers are charged every time someone clicks on their ad. The appearance of their ad (called an "impression") does not cost the advertisers anything. Their ads might appear next to an article on a blog, or they might appear on the Google search results page after someone runs a typical search, but the advertisers will only be charged if someone clicks on their ads.

PPC is an enormous business and it's constantly changing. As of this writing, more than 90 percent of Google's revenue comes from PPC advertising. Yep, that's how they make their money—lots of it. PPC advertising brings exciting opportunities to the world of Internet marketing. In many cases, it is the fastest way to start growing your business immediately. If you are considering using AdWords/PPC for your business, let me give you these three pieces of advice to start with:

- Wade in slowly.
- Do your homework (there is a lot to learn).
- Get help from an expert.

As a PPC specialist myself, I can tell you from experience that nearly everyone who tries to do AdWords themselves ends up wasting a lot of money. When I first started learning about AdWords, I expected to find a fairly simple and straightforward system. What I found was the opposite: a very deep and complex platform. It is also a platform that is constantly changing.

> *Side-note fact*: When you perform a Google search, the AdWords ads (which are the PPC ads) are found on the top and along the right side of the results page. Sometimes they appear on the bottom of the page as well. They are made to look a bit different than the standard (or "organic") listings so that they can be distinguished.

> *Side-note fact*: This part of the book is mostly focused on AdWords; however, I sometimes refer to PPC in general. This is because those principles apply to PPC in general, including on platforms other than AdWords.

Two Simultaneous Goals

With PPC, you have two simultaneous goals:

- Be visible to the people who might actually become customers (based on the words they search, their geographic location, particular times they are searching, etc.)
- Be invisible to everyone else.

Achieving these goals (or at least coming close) requires technical knowledge of the PPC platforms themselves. They have many features meant to streamline your campaigns and costs. Taking advantage of these features is imperative. Also, there is an art and science to PPC. It requires creative use of words, punctuation, and the array of tools you are given to work with. It's a constant battle to both get clicks and avoid clicks.

Should You Use AdWords for Your Business?

Since AdWords is my specialty, you might want to qualify this advice. My opinion is that you should probably use AdWords for your business. The important thing is that you use it in a careful and efficient way, and that's not easy. This is why I highly advise finding a consultant to help you.

The AdWords system is very versatile and flexible. It allows you to take a laser-targeted, conservative approach or a more broad and general one. There are advantages to each. With the narrow, conservative approach, you can be sure your money is spent only on the most likely prospects for your business. With a broader and more liberal one, you can gather more information on which to base your future efforts. A bit of trial-and-error can open up possibilities that are missed by being more conservative.

I managed an AdWords campaign for a stand-up comedian. The business of live comedy is not very well suited to AdWords advertising, because people search the words "comedian" and "stand-up comic" for many different reasons. Most people search those terms to find information about comedians, not to hire one. So we made a very narrowly targeted and conservative campaign. We used the keyword [comedian for hire], formatted as shown here. The brackets indicate a "match type" in AdWords. This match type is called "exact match," and it means that an ad will show only if those exact words are searched, in that exact order, and without any other words before or after. This is an example of how a business can take a conservative and frugal approach to AdWords.

Getting back to the main question of whether or not you should use AdWords for your business: AdWords gives you the opportunity to show up at the top of the Google search results page. The value of this is obviously tremendous. The question is whether your business will make enough income to justify the costs of the clicks. Since I know the versatility and flexibility of AdWords myself, my advice is to use this amazing platform, at least in a low-risk, conservative way.

How to Control Costs

There are two basic ways to control costs in AdWords: daily budgets and keyword bids.

Daily Budgets

When you set up a new campaign, you choose various settings. One crucial setting is the daily budget. This is as simple as it sounds. It's a dollar amount that is not to be exceeded in click costs each day. It gets a little complicated in one way. AdWords will sometimes exceed that amount in a day, but it will compensate on another day to bring your cost average back down. The average length of a month is 30.4 days. AdWords takes your daily budget and multiplies it by 30.4. The resulting number is the maximum cost for that campaign in a month's billing period.

Costs-Per-Click Bids

How much does a click cost? That depends on you. Costs per click are controlled by an auction-based system. You set bids at the campaign, ad group or individual keyword level. The bid you set is the maximum you are willing to pay for a click. When a Google search triggers an appearance of your ad, a split-second auction takes place among those bidding for that keyword at that time and for that location. There is a lot of strategy that goes into bidding. For example, a florist might bid high for the phrase *wedding florist* and low for the phrase *birthday bouquet*.

In the campaign settings you can also select automatic bidding, which means AdWords will decide what to bid for you. In this case, AdWords will automate a process to try to get good results while staying within your daily budget.

The Search Network vs. the Display Network

AdWords consists of two very different types of advertising: search and display. If you plan on using AdWords, it is crucial that you understand the difference. When you set up a new campaign, you are given the choice of using the Search Network, Display Network, or both. Here's an explanation of what those are:

The Google Search Network

The Google Search Network refers to search engines like Google. Advertising on the Search Network means your ads can appear when someone searches for the keywords you designate. So in this situation, people are actually looking for products, services, and information related to a specific topic. To be a little more figurative, they have a question and are looking for an answer. Or, they have a problem and are looking for a solution. This, of course, is what search engines are for. So why is it called the Search Network? Because Google has partners that it has arranged to show its search results with. For example, AOL is in the Google Search Network. If you do a search on AOL, you will get results from the Google search engine.

The Google Display Network

The Google Display Network is very different. The Display Network is a massive inventory of advertising space on pages all over the web. In fact, it's the largest inventory of ad space on the planet. People and businesses that have websites and blogs can "rent out" parts of their web pages for Google advertising. Google shows ads in those spaces and if someone clicks on an ad, the advertiser will pay. Part of the money goes to Google and part of the money goes to the owner of the web page. Google tries to match up ads for certain businesses to the content the ads appear with. For example, a travel agent who runs an AdWords display ad might have their ad appear next to a news article about airline prices or specific destinations like Paris, London, or Las Vegas. Advertisers also have the option of choosing specific pages on specific websites to show their ads. This is done by setting up a campaign on the Display Network, choosing placement targeting for specific web pages, and then bidding for the space.

Account Levels and Structure

There are different levels in the AdWords system. An important part of using AdWords is understanding functions and settings that go with the different levels. The levels of AdWords are (from the top down): account, campaign, ad group, and keyword (or placement on the Display Network). Accounts can have multiple campaigns, campaigns can have multiple ad groups, and ad groups can have multiple keywords (and/or placements). Here is a brief description of the functions and settings that relate to the different levels:

Account Level

Most of the settings in AdWords are at lower levels, but a few settings are made at the account level, such as billing, address, language, account access, notification settings, and preferences.

Campaign Level

To have a functioning AdWords account, you must have at least one campaign, one ad group, one keyword or placement, and one ad. The first step after opening an AdWords account is creating a campaign. When you create a campaign, you will decide on various settings such as:

- Whether the campaign will run on the Search Network, Display Network, or both. You can also set it to only run on the Google search engine.

- Whether you want to specify particular devices to target (such as mobile phones, or tablets).

- What the daily budget for the campaign will be.

- What geographic areas the campaign will cover – they can be countries, states, cities, congressional districts, zip codes, or a radius around a particular address.

- Whether the campaign will turn on and off on a schedule—for example, if you sell NBA jerseys online, you may only want your ads to show during certain NBA games.

Ad Group Level

After creating a campaign, you will need to create at least one ad group within that campaign. Ad groups are where your keywords and actual ads reside. The purpose of ad groups is to keep a tight theme that directly relates the designated keywords to the actual ad that shows, and (finally) to the landing page the ad will lead to. For an example of a good use of ad groups: an expert mechanic might have one ad group for auto repair and another for motorcycle repair. The only reason to create separate campaigns for different ventures would be to control the daily budgets separately, or to have different campaign settings (such as geographical areas covered, or ad scheduling).

If you are running a display campaign, you might wish to use placements without any keywords. This simply means that you choose specific web pages on specific websites where you want your ads to show. You create an appropriate ad for that space, which can be a text ad, an image ad, or possibly a video ad. Then you set a bid for having your ad show on that web page.

Some of the functions and settings found at the ad group level are:

- Ad group level bid. This will be the default bid for every keyword and placement in the ad group. These bids can be overridden by setting different bids at the keyword or placement level.

- Keywords. Here you will add the keywords that will trigger your ad.

- Ad creation. Here you will create the actual ad that will run. You can also create more than one ad and set the ads to rotate (thereby split-testing to see which ad performs better).

Keyword (or Placement) Level

At the keyword or placement level, you designate the actual keyword (for keyword targeting on the Search Network or contextual targeting on the Display Network) or place you want your ad to show on a particular web page. You can also set a bid for each keyword or placement that will override the bid set at the campaign or ad group level.

Keyword Match Types

One of the most brilliant aspects of AdWords is the system of match types that can be used for keywords. Match types give you a greater degree of control to determine which searches should trigger the appearance of your ad. For example, if you designate the keyword blue flannel pajamas to trigger your ad, do you want your ad to be displayed if the searcher adds another word in the phrase, like cheap blue flannel pajamas? Or what if they search your keywords in a different order, like flannel pajamas blue? By setting various match types, you can control issues like these. It takes time and practice to learn the techniques that fully utilize the power of the match types, but it is a crucial aspect of AdWords. Here is a brief description of each match type:

Broad Match

As its name suggests, broad match allows for the broadest interpretation of search queries. To use a keyword in this match type, simply type the keyword without any formatting around it.

> *Warning:* Avoid using broad match. It is too broad and can run up your costs very quickly. A great many of the clicks you receive will likely be off-target for your business. For example, setting the keyword *dancing shoes* to broad match might trigger your ad for the search *dancing cruise*. If you are going to use broad match, consider it a temporary experiment to educate yourself on the different ways people search your keywords. You can use that information to get ideas for new keywords and approaches.

Modified Broad Match

The next most broadly interpreted match type is modified broad match. This is a very handy and important match type that has only been around for a couple of years. It gives you much more control than broad match, but allows flexibility as well. To use this match type, simply put a plus (+) sign before each keyword that must be part of a search query. For example, the keyword +valentines roses +bouquet indicates that the searcher must use the words valentines and bouquet in the search query. The word roses is not as mandatory. Also, the words can be in any order. If someone searches for bouquet for valentines day, it would still most likely trigger the ad.

Phrase Match

Phrase match is a more rigidly controlled match type because it requires that the entire keyword phrase appears in the proper order. To use phrase match, simply put quotation marks around the whole keyword phrase. The keyword "vegetarian cooking classes" indicates that the searcher must use that phrase in order to trigger the ad. Although this match type is more rigid, it does allow the searcher to use additional words before and after the keyword phrase. For example, the search query vegetarian cooking classes springfield il would still trigger the ad.

Exact Match

The most precise and rigid keyword match type is exact match. Exact match gives you complete control over what searches will trigger your ad because it requires that the search query matches your keyword exactly. It requires that it be those exact words, in that exact order, and without any words before or after. If you want to use AdWords in a very frugal and conservative way, consider having several different keywords in exact match. You could even have several hundred keywords in exact match if you want to laser-target your approach this way. I would not recommend this in most cases, but it is an option. To use exact match, simply put brackets around the keyword phrase like this [keyword phrase].

Negative

As I mentioned above, negative keywords are a crucial cost-saving component of AdWords. By designating words as negative keywords, you can prevent the showing of your ad. For example, if a photographer does studio portraits but not outdoor portraits, they can set "outdoor" and "nature" to be negative keywords. This way, their ad can be displayed for the search "portraits" but not for the search "outdoor portraits." It is important to have an ever-expanding list of negative keywords. By looking at the Search Terms Report in AdWords, you can see the actual searches people make that lead to clicks on your ad. This is usually a goldmine for finding new negatives to use. But just to get you started, consider using the words free, cheap, discount, and reviews as negative keywords for your account. To add keywords as negatives, simply put a negative (-) sign before the keyword. (Also, there is a designated place where negative keywords can be added without the need for any formatting.)

Match type strategies

If your goal is to experiment (which is a good goal at first), use the less-rigidly controlled modified broad match. This will lead to more impressions of your ad than phrase or exact match. More impressions allow you to glean more about what's happening and how to proceed. You can then consider these questions: Are your ads getting clicks? If so, what are the search terms people use that lead to a click? If they are not getting many clicks, is it because your ad is showing too low on the results page? (Raising your bid can help in this situation.) Or perhaps the wording of your ad is not appealing to the searchers? The broader your keywords are, the more impressions you will get. The more impressions you get, the more data you will have for making judgments. It is still a good idea to avoid broad match, however. If you're going to use it, do so with a low daily budget and a careful watch. If your goal is to make every penny count, lean more toward phrase and exact match. This means your ad won't show as much for irrelevant searches.

Using the same keywords in multiple match types

Can you use the same keywords in multiple match types at once? Yes, you can and you should. Seems weird, right? After all, won't they be competing against each other within the same ad group? Yes, they will compete against each other sometimes, but you can predetermine who the winner will be by setting different bids for each (I told you this takes time and practice!) Here's how it works… If you add these keywords to your ad group +cowboy +boots, "cowboy boots" and [cowboy boots], and then someone searches the words cowboy boots, AdWords must determine which keyword is going to trigger the ad. It will weigh different variables, including the bids for each keyword. As the advertiser, it is advantageous to bid highest for the exact match version, then lower for the phrase match version, and then lower still for the modified broad match version. This is because the more rigid the match type is, the more we can closely discern what the searcher is looking for. After all, there is a big difference between the query cowboy boots and the query cowboy boots for pets. Bidding highest for exact match is safer because it doesn't allow for additional words that change the meaning. And bidding higher for phrase match over modified broad match is safer because it requires a particular phrase to appear in the search query and not a variation that changes the order of the words, or adds others within. (To use these strategies, you must choose "manual bidding" in the campaign settings.)

> *Side-note fact*: When keyword phrases are long, they are described as having a "long tail." For example, the keyword *tuxedos for rent* is not a long-tail keyword. To make it a longer-tail keyword, we could change it to *tuxedos for rent in cincinatti*. To make it a very long tail keyword, we could make it *white wool tuxedos for rent in cincinatti in kids sizes*. Using long-tail keywords can sometimes give us an advantage on AdWords or in SEO (search engine optimization).

Terms to Understand

Here is a little glossary of important terms to understand in AdWords and other PPC platforms. These are all basic terms and concepts you must know to understand the AdWords interface and the fundamental principles of PPC.

Impression – The appearance of an ad.

CTR – "Click-through-rate" is the number of clicks on an ad divided by the number of impressions of an ad. If an ad gets 1000 impressions and 10 clicks, the CTR would be 1%. Google considers a 1% CTR to be healthy. A higher CTR could be a good or bad thing, depending on how much new business/revenue is generated from the clicks. (In the end, profit for your business is the most important metric.)

AdWords/Pay-Per-Click

Landing Page – The landing page is simply the web page a person will be taken to if they click on your ad. This is something you determine when setting the "destination URL" in the ad creation process.

Quality Score – Google assigns a "quality score" to each keyword you are bidding on. This is a computerized evaluation of various factors, such as historical performance of the keyword, historical performance of the ad group, the CTR of the keyword, the relevance of the words in the ad, the relevance of the landing page to the keyword, and more. Your quality score can be positively or negatively affected by the way you use the AdWords system, but it works somewhat mysteriously. It is important, however, because it directly affects the costs-per-click and the ranking order of the ads on a search results page. (To see the quality score for your keywords, go to the "keywords" tab and customize the columns to show quality score.)

Rank/Position – The ad at the very top of the page is in position one. The next ad is in position two, and so forth. In the AdWords interface, you can see the "average position" of your campaigns, ad groups, keywords, and ads.

Search Term/Query – Search terms (or queries) refer to the terms used by the person doing the search. For example, *bookstore in canton ohio* might be what someone searches on Google. AdWords allows you to see the actual terms used that triggered your ads in the search terms report. This is enormously helpful for seeing whether your keywords and match types are on target.

Placement – A placement is when a display ad shows on a web page somewhere. For example, if you are using the Google Display Network in AdWords, your ad might show next to an article on a news website or next to a blog article.

Contextual targeting – Contextual targeting is one way that the Google Display Network places your ad on web pages. It uses the keywords you designate to align your ads with relevant web content.

Conversion – A conversion is when someone performs a desired action on a web page, such as making a purchase, visiting a particular page on your site, or opting in to receive your email newsletter. Conversion tracking can be set up in AdWords to show the rate at which your visitors are converting. This is helpful for you to track the results of changes you might want to experiment with. For example, you might compare the results between two ad variations to see which lead to more conversions.

Other Major PPC Platforms

Google gets the lion's share of search engine traffic these days, but don't count out other PPC platforms for advertising. Here are a few other services that offer PPC advertising.

Bing/Yahoo (www.bingads.microsoft.com)

>The Bing and Yahoo search engines have a partnership and provide the same search results (which are actually powered by Bing). Although not as popular as Google, these search engines still get quite a bit of traffic. If you want to use the Google AdWords platform for PPC action, there is no reason not to use Bing Ads as well. It functions very similarly to AdWords. In fact, it has a feature that lets you import your AdWords campaigns directly into its system. This is very handy. There are some differences from AdWords, especially in where you go to change certain settings. Some settings are changeable at the campaign level and some are changeable at the ad group level, depending on which system you are using. For the most part, however, AdWords and BingAds do the same thing. If you run PPC ads on both, you will cover roughly 94% of the search market. BingAds is also known to have lower costs per click.

Facebook advertising (www.facebook.com/ads/)

>For several years, Facebook has offered a PPC platform. Facebook's platform is based on display ads, which are very different than search result ads. Facebook ads appear on the right side as people look at news feed posts from their friends. To succeed at this type of advertising, ads need to be very enticing. After all, what's going to take your attention away from reading posts and looking at

photos from your friends, let alone lead you toward making some kind of purchase?

The great benefit of Facebook PPC is that they have a wealth of personal knowledge about their users, such as what movies they like, what bands they like, what sports they like, etc. This can be extremely valuable to businesses that sell to a small niche market. For example, if your business sells a book about unusual gardening techniques, you can target your ad to be displayed only to those who have listed gardening as one of their interests.

Facebook is still fairly new in the PPC arena and their system is still coming of age. Their interface is quite easy to use, though, and shows many of the same metrics seen in AdWords. If you decide to try Facebook Ads, remember that it is display advertising and that your ads need to be very enticing to attract attention.

(*See more about using Facebook for business in Part 5 of this book*)

Twitter advertising (www.ads.twitter.com)

Twitter is also a relative newcomer to the PPC arena, but it offers interesting approaches to PPC advertising. One program it offers is "Promoted Tweets." This is where you create a tweet and set it to be seen at the top of your followers' timelines. You will then be charged if someone clicks to take one of the following actions: re-tweet, reply, add to favorites, or click to your profile. You can target promoted tweets to occur within a specified geographic area, by particular device, by interests, by gender, or by similarity to existing followers.

Twitter's other PPC feature is called "Promoted Accounts." Promoted Accounts is intended to help you increase your follower count. This will cause your account to be prominently displayed in the Who to Follow section of your Twitter page. You are charged only when a user follows you. Like promoted tweets, you can target promoted accounts to occur within a specified geographic area, by particular device, by interests, by gender, or by similarity to existing followers.

(*See more about Twitter for business in Part 5 of this book*)

LinkedIn advertising (www.linkedin.com/advertising/)

LinkedIn has its own pay-per-click ad system for reaching out to other members. The ads can appear in two different places: on the sidebar or at the top of the site. They include a photo, a 25-character headline and a 75-character description. You can target your ads by industry, job function, group, geography, age, and more. You can also split-test ads to see which get a better response.

(*See more about LinkedIn in Part 5 of this book*)

Summary

Most important things to know from this section:

- Google AdWords provides a method of placing ads that can be highly visible on search results pages.
- AdWords is primarily a PPC (pay-per-click) platform, meaning advertisers only pay when someone clicks on their ad.
- PPC advertising requires having two simultaneous goals: visibility to the searchers who are more likely to become customers and invisibility to everyone else.
- There are two ways to control costs in AdWords: by setting daily budgets for your campaigns and by setting maximum cost-per-click bids for your campaigns, ad groups, or individual keywords.
- There is a huge difference between search and display advertising. The AdWords platform gives you the option to use either or both.
- Learning to use the keyword match types is an invaluable skill to help streamline your costs in AdWords.
- If you are using AdWords, you can get more visibility by importing your campaigns into BingAds. This will make your ads visible on both the Bing and Yahoo search engines.

AdWords/Pay-Per-Click

Most important things to do:

- Start slowly with AdWords and learn to understand the results of your account activity.

- Find a consultant to assist you as you go. A consultant can advise you in ways that will prevent wasted money in your campaigns.

- Look at the search terms report. This report is very instructive for letting you know if you are attracting the right kind of searchers.

- Remember that the broad match types will waste more money, but will yield data that can be useful for targeting and streamlining later.

- Remember that the more conservative match types (like exact and phrase) will keep your costs more streamlined, but give you less data to learn and get ideas from.

- Always add as many negative keywords as possible to streamline your costs. Use the search terms report to get ideas for new negatives.

- Make sure your ad groups are tightly themed around a specific topic.

- Split-test to constantly improve your ads.

Most important things NOT to do:

- Use the Display Network in AdWords, unless you really know what you are doing.

- Use broad match keywords, unless it is a short-term experiment to learn from.

- Set your daily budgets too high in the beginning.

- Spend money on clicks without getting help, and without knowing what you are doing.

- Ignore the importance of having a good landing page. Even if your AdWords campaigns are healthy, it still takes a good landing page to get a customer or conversion.

Part 4-Search Engine Optimization (SEO)

Search engine optimization (aka SEO) is the process of making web pages rank higher and more visibly on the search engine results pages—or at least attempting to do so. SEO strategies are based on keywords that people might search. For example, if your business sells batteries for video cameras, you would want to optimize for the keyword phrase batteries for video cameras, or video camera batteries. By doing this, your web pages will hopefully be highly visible when people search those or similar terms on a search engine.

How valuable is SEO? If your business regularly appears at the top of Google search result pages, the answer is probably "very valuable." Unlike pay-per-click ads, there is no cost when someone clicks on a link to your website. Many businesses have thrived and many fortunes have been made as a result of SEO. A tremendous amount of free traffic to your website can come from good optimization, and that can lead to many new customers.

> *Side-note fact*: The standard (non-PPC) listings on a search results page are called the "organic" listings. They are displayed in the main body of the results page, while the PPC ads are shown on the top and along the right side. The main purpose of the search engines is to give organic listings; however, this doesn't lead to any revenue for the search engine companies. That's why they created PPC platforms like AdWords.

How Search Engines Provide Results to Searches

Amazing, isn't it? You search for something on Google, Yahoo or Bing and you are immediately given results that match what you're looking for. It seems like they have that list ready before you even search, doesn't it? Well, in a way they do. Search engines have enormous indexes of web pages. They are constantly adding more and more pages every day. They know where the pages are located, how long they have been there, what the pages are about, and other information. How do they know? Because they have special computers that are constantly crawling the web. These computers are called "spiders." They crawl and crawl and crawl, endlessly following links. As they find new pages, they look for key information that indicates what the pages are about. The information is then added to the index. Whenever someone wants information about something, the search engines refer to that index to find answers and results.

Search engine technology has improved over time. The search engine companies want to provide a good experience to their users, so they are constantly improving and tweaking their systems. They strive to provide relevant, accurate and high-quality results. Each search engine has its own formula (or algorithm, to be precise) that creates the results you see when you do a search. Google's algorithm compares over 200 factors when it decides which web pages to display in its search results, and in what ranking order. As the web gets larger and more sophisticated, search engines need to invent ways to keep up.

> *Side-note fact*: Google's web crawler is called the "Googlebot."

Is There a Cost to SEO Traffic?

Some would say there is no cost for SEO traffic because there is no charge to be indexed by the search engines or when someone clicks on a link from a search results page. I would say yes, however, because SEO can be very hard work. How difficult is it to rank high for your business? It all depends on the competition. If your business is selling life insurance on a national level, good luck. Just imagine how competitive that market is. If your business is selling roller-skates for squirrels in Tempe, Arizona, your SEO efforts would succeed much more easily. After all, how many web pages can there be for selling roller-skates for squirrels in Tempe, Arizona? (Maybe there are more than I realize. I admit I didn't even check.)

The cost of SEO is the time invested in it. Of course, there is a large industry of SEO professionals who can do the work for you. Even Fortune 500 companies invest heavily in hiring SEO professionals. Perhaps you will want to hire a professional to help you, but be warned: if the wrong methods are used, your site can be penalized by the search engines. People always have and always will try to manipulate search engine results. These days, it's very difficult to accomplish. Just like gambling in a Las Vegas casino: you can try to cheat, but they are very good at catching you. This can cause you to be banned—and you don't want that to happen with one of the major search engines.

White-hat & Black-hat SEO

In SEO parlance, white-hat describes SEO performed in a proper and legitimate way. This means adding quality content that people will actually want to read or see. Adding quality content to your website causes people to spend more time looking at your pages, and they may decide to link from their website to yours. These actions don't go unnoticed by the search engines. They are telling signs that your website is providing a quality experience to its visitors. Besides adding quality content, there are other measures to take that are important and considered white-hat. (These measures are mentioned later in this section.)

Black-hat SEO means just what you think: trying to manipulate and cheat the system. There are hundreds, maybe thousands of ways people have figured out to get their sites to rank higher. It is a never-ending struggle for the black-hatters. They are determined to find a shortcut for ranking higher. Unfortunately for them, however, it has become extremely difficult to do. And if black-hat methods are detected, the page will be penalized with a lower ranking, or by being banned altogether.

One black-hat method of the past was to have a keyword typed in thousands of times on the same web page. The search engines index how many times certain words appear on pages in order to glean what the pages are about. If the word bicycle appears fifty-seven times on a page, the search engine might determine that the page has something to do with bicycles. When search engines were less sophisticated, they were tricked by people putting certain keywords hundreds or thousands of times on the same web page. This might have looked very strange if the visitor of the page saw the repetition—but they didn't. The designer would simply make the repetitive keyword the same color as the page background, and voila! The repetitions of the keyword were visible to the search engine spiders but invisible to viewers of the web page.

Search Engine Optimization (SEO)

Most SEO professionals now agree that the search engines have won the war over the black-hatters. There is little to do now, other than stick with proper white-hat methods. The interesting thing is that it's not easy to define exactly where the line is between white-hat and black-hat SEO. There is no official guidebook. A good policy, however, is to concentrate on creating quality content for your website users rather than creating content with search engine spiders in mind.

On-Page & Off-Page SEO

Aside from the white-hat and black-hat classifications, there are two kinds of SEO: on-page and off-page.

> On-page SEO refers to things that can be directly controlled on your website. Some of the things, such as headings and paragraphs of text, appear visible to viewers of your pages. Other things are tucked away in the underlying code, and not meant to be visible to viewers of the page.

> Off-page SEO involves trying to gain notice for your web pages from other places on the web. Since search engine spiders crawl pages all over the web, they notice where there are links and references to other websites. If the spiders see that your pages are mentioned or linked to on other reputable web pages, your rankings will be favorably influenced.

On-Page Optimization

There are things you can do on your own web pages that go a long way for SEO. Not only is it okay to do these things, the search engines want you to them. Remember that search engine spiders will crawl your site, looking for hints about the subject of your web pages. The following items are key indicators. Make sure you carefully decide on the keywords you use for on-page optimization. Here are some places where search engine spiders look on your pages:

Page Title

The page title is what shows in the top of the browser window or tab when a web page is loaded. This is perhaps the most important thing to be optimized with keywords. The title is placed between html tags within the header-section of the html document with the page code. How you set the title depends on what method you're using to build your web pages.

Meta Description

This is another tag that's placed in the header section of the html document with the page code. The text placed here is often seen on search engine results pages to describe what the web page is about.

Headings

Headings (H1 and H2 tags in html) are a key indicator for the search engine spiders to decipher the content on a web page.

Paragraph Text

Search engines examine the text on web pages to look for words that appear frequently, indicating the subject matter of the web page.

Alt-Tags

When you have images on your web pages, it's highly advisable to have alt-tags (meaning "alternative tags") that indicate what's shown in the images. This is important for times when images might not load into a browser (the alt-tags words will show instead) and it also gives another opportunity to further optimize your page with keywords.

Navigational Links

The links and the anchor text for links are noticed by the search engine spiders. Make sure to use words that relate to the relevant subjects.

Search Engine Optimization (SEO)

URL

Having keywords directly in the URL can be an effective optimization technique as well. For example, if I create a page about skateboard tricks on my website, I can create the following URL for that page: www.brickway.net/skateboard-tricks/.

The most important on-page SEO method is to provide quality content that will interest your visitors. The more, the better. Having a blog is a great way to keep a fresh stream of content flowing in your site. Use keywords in your blog posts that are relevant to your business. This is perhaps the most effective method of SEO. (There is more about blogging in Part 2 of this book.)

Off-Page Optimization

When you're talking about off-page SEO, you are mostly talking about backlinks. Backlinks are links to your website from other sites. For quite some time, backlinks have been used by the search engines to observe the popularity of different web pages. For example, if a certain web page has a high number of links to it from around the web, the search engines assume that there must be good content on that web page. That page will likely get better rankings than pages with similar content that don't have as many backlinks to it. It started out as a simple concept: the more backlinks, the better for ranking. Then things changed. The black-hatters have been all over this for years. A whole industry sprouted up, just to create massive amounts of links to websites—for a price. Enterprising black-hatters created "link farms," which are low-quality websites created solely for the purpose of selling links to paying customers. Needless to say, the search engines caught on. Nowadays, they can tell the difference between high- and low-quality backlinks.

Search engine indexes use sophisticated methods to determine the quality and credibility of web pages, including yours. If a page with good credibility links to your website, that will reflect favorably on you. If a page with low credibility links to your site, it would not result in better rankings for you. (It could actually result in a penalty, especially if it's from a link farm.)

Another important aspect of backlinks has to do with relevance. If backlinks come from web pages that seem to be from the same field or a similar topic, that increases their value. For example, if your web page is about country line-dancing and a web page about country music festivals links to your page, that makes it a highly relevant backlink. On the other hand, if your web page is about country line-dancing and a website about carbon emissions testing links to your page, that's not a very relevant backlink, and its value is decreased.

Now that you know what backlinks are, how they can be important, and how they can have varying degrees of impact, I'll explain a few sub-topics related to backlink quality. These are: PageRank, anchor text, link juice, reciprocal/one-way links, and "no-follow"/"do-follow" links.

PageRank

PageRank is Google's proprietary system for grading web pages on their apparent strength and credibility. It's named after one of the co-founders of Google, Larry Page. All web pages are given a PageRank number from zero to ten. Although the formula for creating the PageRank number is top-secret, certain aspects of it are common knowledge. Here are a few things known to have an effect:

- Number and quality of backlinks to that web page
- Age of the domain name (When a domain name is newly registered, it is believed to have a PageRank disadvantage for a while. SEO professionals call this "being in the Google sandbox.")
- The content of the webpage
- Internal website links
- Keyword density (i.e., how often certain words appear in the text of the web pages)

Why is PageRank important when it comes to backlinks? Because the value of a backlink is related to the PageRank of the page doing the linking. The higher the PageRank on that page, the more beneficial the backlink is for rankings.

Anchor text

Anchor text is the actual text that becomes a clickable hyperlink. It's often underlined and in blue, but that depends on the styling of the web page you are on. When it comes to the value of backlinks, search engines pay close attention to the anchor text of links. They consider it to be a telling sign about the subject of the page the link is pointing to. For example, if the anchor text is "click here for free legal advice," those words will help determine how the page linked to will be indexed. If there is a common theme to the keywords in anchor text, that is a good thing for ranking. If a web page has a lot of backlinks, but the anchor text is not consistent, the impact of the backlinks won't be as significant.

When SEO professionals attempt to build backlinks, they are careful about ensuring that the anchor text reflects the subjects and keywords of the pages to which they are linking. Be warned, though. Nowadays it's important that the anchor text NOT BE exactly the same on every backlink. Search engines try to reward natural activity on the web and to punish efforts to manipulate rankings. If you have a popular web page, truly natural backlinks would probably have varying anchor text. Large numbers of backlinks with exactly the same anchor text appear more like an SEO campaign than natural web activity. In the ideal situation, backlinks will have anchor text that reflects a consistent theme or topic, but not be identical in wording.

Link juice

Link juice is another term that relates to the power of a backlink. It basically means "link power." When a web page has a large number of links on it, the power of each link gets diluted. There is a big difference to having five links on a web page and five hundred. If a person puts five hundred links on one web page, it would appear that this page owner is indiscriminate about who he or she links to. The search engines take notice of this and determine the significance of the links accordingly.

Reciprocal/One-way

Reciprocal linking is when there are mutual links between two web pages. For example, if you are a house painter and your friend is a plumber, you might agree to give each other a link from your own websites. One-way linking simply means that the link goes only one way—i.e., it's not reciprocated. The value of a one-way link is generally better than that of a reciprocal one.

No follow/Do follow

"No follow" and "do follow" are coded signs for search engine spiders. They can sometimes be found in the html coding of hyperlinks. Here is an example of the "no follow" tag in html code:

<a href="http://www.hankslingerie.com" rel="nofollow">Anchor Text</a>

The "no follow" indicates that certain information normally associated with backlinks should be ignored by the search engines. In the case of Google, that means PageRank and anchor text. If neither the "no follow" or "do follow" tag appears, it becomes a "do follow" link by default. Assigning the "no follow" tag is a bit like saying, "we are linking to this web page, but are not really vouching for the credibility of this web page."

Methods for Building Backlinks

If you are serious about SEO, finding ways to build backlinks is an important task. Though this can be a time-consuming and laborious process, good backlinks can be great for your rankings in the search engines. Here are a few ways you might consider to drum up backlinks to your web pages:

Complimentary businesses (reciprocal links)

Do you know anyone who has a website with whom you could exchange links? A reciprocal backlink could have some value and could also bring you traffic and customers. This technique becomes more valuable if there is a similarity in the topics of your web pages.

Search Engine Optimization (SEO)

Article marketing

One of the most prominent methods of backlink building in recent years is article marketing. This is generally how it works: First, you write an article about a topic related to your business. Then you submit it to be published on another website. To get a backlink, you simply add a link to your website from the article itself. There are hundreds of article-submission sites that allow you to submit articles in this fashion. Although this can still be an effective way to get backlinks, it is not as beneficial to SEO as it once was. The search engines have devalued this type of link because it's been an over-used tactic to influence rankings. If you are going to pursue article marketing for backlinks, be sure to submit your articles to sites that appear more credible and less spammy.

Guest posting

Guest posting is like article marketing, but it is directed more at blogs. Many blog owners are constantly trying to add good content to their blogs. If you can provide an article or some other content that they can use, you can often get a quality backlink to your web site. It's important that there is a good match between the topic of your article and the main topic of the blog. It's also important that it be a quality blog site, and not one that's full of junky and spammy content. If you want to write guest posts for bloggers, simply contact the blog owners and ask if they would be interested in that arrangement.

Write a review of another business on your website

If you offer something beneficial to another business owner, perhaps they will be willing to link to your website. One idea is to write a favorable article, review, or blurb about a business on your site and then suggest that they link to it. Again, it helps more if there is some similarity or relevant connection between the businesses.

Forums

Around the web, there are many forums where people of a similar interest post questions and information. There are forums for almost any topic you can imagine. Participating in these forums is one way to get good backlinks. It's important to use this method with the intention of making a real contribution to the group. Forums have moderators that are on the lookout for those who are only trying to score a good backlink. To find forums on various topics go to Google.com and search "forum: your topic."

Press releases

Creating content that could be newsworthy is one way of attempting to get backlinks. Writing an article in the form of a press release, and then distributing it to various press release gathering sites could lead to the article getting picked up and published. That process can sometimes result in good backlinks.

Blog comments

At the bottom of many blog articles there is a place to leave comments from the readers. Commenting on blog articles can be a way to get backlinks. Usually these are "no follow" links, but they can still have value. You definitely would want to find blogs about a topic related to your business that get a decent amount of traffic. Beware, though: there are a lot of black-hatters out there constantly spamming article-comment fields. This is known as "comment spam." It's not very effective because blog owners can easily remove these types of comments. However, blog owners usually appreciate real comments from people who actually read their articles. You can sometimes manage to get a backlink from comments you make.

About Keywords

The most fundamental thing to do for SEO is choose the keywords for which you want to optimize. This step might seem like a simple and quick one, but there can be more to it than you realize. There are several key questions to consider such as:

- What search phrases are most commonly used related to my business?
- How competitive are those keywords?
- What keywords can I use to distinguish myself from the competition?

The process of choosing keywords should not be rushed, since it's the foundation of all of your SEO efforts. SEO success sometimes comes from adding the right "tail" to your keywords. As I mentioned in Part 3 of this book, adding words to more narrowly define your main keywords is called "adding to the tail." A keyword such as coffee cups is considered short-tail. A keyword such as coffee cups with holiday designs is long-tail. Since there is so much competition on the web, long-tail keywords can be your best method of standing out..

When it comes to finding out how competitive certain keywords are, there are valuable tools you can (and should) use. One such tool is the Google Keyword Planner. It can provide a wealth of information for your keyword research. To use it, you must open an AdWords account (which is free to do).

Other keyword tools:
>www.bing.com/toolbox/keywords/
>www.wordtracker.com
>www.ubersuggest.org

Should You Use SEO for Your Business?

Many businesses have reaped big profits as a result of SEO. Is it right for your business? My opinion is that it probably is, at least to some degree. For sure, you should do simple on-page optimization, such as setting the page titles, meta description tags, and headings to reflect the subject of each web page. The best long-term strategy is to continuously create great content. With great content, you shouldn't need to put much effort into building backlinks. People like to link to pages that have great content. Gaining backlinks can happen naturally. Having a blog is usually the best way to keep your site fresh and full of great content. Each blog post can have different topics, keywords, and keyword variations related to your business to help with SEO.

A Constantly Moving Goalpost

There are some things you can always count on with SEO, and one of those things is change. As the black-hatters invent more ways to manipulate the search results, the search engines modify their algorithms to counter those efforts. Also, the technology is constantly changing, which means more and different factors will be involved in the future than are now. A simple change in a search engine algorithm can demote a web page from position one on the search results page to position eighty-two, without any prior warning. But if you concentrate your SEO efforts on having great quality content, you are better positioned for long-term success with your rankings.

SEO Tools

There are a number of tools and services available to help with your SEO efforts. They can give you valuable information to guide and track your progress. Some of the statistics you can examine from these tools are: PageRank, number of backlinks, types of backlinks, web page rankings, website comparisons, and traffic information. You can examine these statistics for your own web pages and websites or for others as well, including ones owned by your competition.

www.tools.seobook.com
www.hubspot.com
www.raventools.com
www.majesticseo.com
www.opensiteexplorer.org

SEARCH ENGINE OPTIMIZATION (SEO)

SEO for Local

In Part 2, I mentioned that the search engines have a separate system designed especially for listing local businesses. This can be a very valuable way to get exposure in your local area, and it is free. Taking advantage of the local listings offered by the major search engines is one of best ways to grow your local business from Internet marketing.

The first step for showing in the local listings is to register your business with the search engines. After submitting the information, there will be a verification process to prove that the business is located where you say it is. Once you have successfully registered and verified your business, the next step is to try to rank higher on the results pages.

Just like ranking for organic results, the search engines have special algorithms for the local results. These algorithms rank many different factors. Although the actual algorithms are not disclosed, there is a lot of information that has been made available to get us headed in the right direction..

Here are some of the factors known to affect the rankings. Applying some SEO attention to these factors is a good investment of time.

- **Information on your business page.** When you register your local business, you give information and descriptions about your business. Be sure to categorize your business accurately and use your most important keywords in prominent places. Also, make sure to complete your business profile as much as possible, including adding photos.

- **Reviews.** Reviews are becoming a much bigger part of how people hire local businesses. The number and quality of reviews your business page receives also contributes as a ranking factor.

- **Backlinks.** Just like with standard SEO, backlinks are important. Having them point to your website is good. Also try to get a few that point directly to your Google+ business page. In fact, linking your own website to your Google+ business page is a great idea.

- **Citations.** Building citations, or "mentions," of your business around the web is a major factor in the local rankings. As I mentioned in Part 2, it is very important to have a consistent NAP (name address and phone number) in your citations. There are many kinds of citations and various ways to build them, but definitely start with major directory sites like www.yellowbook.com and www.supermedia.com. (To see a more extensive list of sites for building citations, go to www.brickway.net/building-citations/.)

Summary

Most important things to know from this section:

- SEO (search engine optimization) is the process of making your web pages rank higher on search results pages, or at least attempting to do so.

- Creating quality content is a mainstay of SEO. If you can provide quality content, it will likely result in more traffic to your web pages, higher rankings with the search engines, and (one would hope) more customers.

- "White-hat" is the term used to describe legitimate SEO tactics.

- "Black-hat" is the term used to describe trying to manipulate the search engines in order to receive higher rankings.

- "On-page SEO" refers to things you can do to optimize the content and code of your web pages.

- "Off-page SEO" refers to processes external to your website, such as finding ways to get backlinks.

- "Backlinks" are links to your web pages from other pages on the web. Tracking backlinks is a method the search engines use to gauge the popularity and significance of pages on the web. Backlinks can be a major factor in determining web page rankings by the search engines.

- SEO is generally a page thing, not a site thing. Think of each page of your site as being separate, then use SEO tactics to optimize them individually.

Search Engine Optimization (SEO)

Most important things to do:

- Commit to only white-hat tactics. For the long run, it's the only way. Create a great website that is useful for its visitors. That alone is a great SEO strategy.

- Make sure each page you want to show in search results has on-page optimization, such as page titles, the description meta tag, alternative text for photos, and formatted headings above blocks of text.

- If you are serious about SEO, start finding ways to get quality backlinks. Doing guest posting on blogs, participating in forums, and asking people you know for links are ways to get started.

- If you are serious about SEO, you should definitely have a blog, and continuously add content that can be helpful for your visitors. Quality blog postings can lead to higher rankings, more traffic, and natural backlinks to your site.

Most important things NOT to do:

- Waste time trying to manipulate the search engines.

- Overlook the importance of adding basic on-page optimization, especially the <title> tag. The title tag is one of the most important places a web spider looks to know the topic of a web page.

- Hire someone to create backlinks for you without knowing exactly what their tactics are. Links from link farms and other low-quality sites can only harm your rankings.

- Rush the process of keyword research. All of your time and effort on SEO will be based on your keyword research. Carefully consider options for standing out from the competition, such as adding a longer tail to your keywords.

Part 5-The Social Web for Business

The biggest change on the web in the last several years has been the explosive growth of social websites. Facebook, Twitter, LinkedIn, Google+ and others have become regular parts of daily life for millions of people. On these enormous networks, people share photos, videos, and written messages. Mobile devices, such as smartphones and tablets, have made it much easier for us to continuously post and get information from friends, family, groups, organizations and businesses. In case you haven't noticed yet, the social web is a game-changer for large and small businesses alike.

This change is not good news for everyone. Even though the social web represents a low-cost opportunity to market your business, there are those of us who just don't want to do it (sound familiar?). Not everyone is the "tweeting" type, or the type who constantly wants to show photos to everyone they know. For those who are resisting the trend of using the social web for business, the bad news only gets worse. Not only is the social web here to stay, it's only going to get more pervasive in our lives. Your competitors are going to use it. You need to as well.

So what are small business owners to do? What is the key to jumping on the social web bandwagon successfully? In a word, the key is: engagement. When you have an account on one of the major social networks, you can easily connect with people you know. You can also connect with people you don't know. It's more or less like going to a party: you have to show up, look presentable, and be part of the conversation. This includes both sharing information and paying attention to the posts of others. Each of the major social networks has its own features and protocols, but they are all similar in some ways as well. The good news is that there are no hard and fast rules about how to go about using the social web. You can start slow and then proceed at the pace with which you feel comfortable. The important thing is that you and your business are a part of it. To use a metaphor: the train is leaving the station, and you need to be on it.

In this section, I will explain the most important things you need to know about using the four largest social websites: Facebook, Twitter, LinkedIn and Google+. Each site has over one hundred million users, and offers various methods for businesses to market their products or services. They all have aspects that can get confusing and complicated, but they can also be used in a simple and easy way that takes advantage of their most basic functionality. In my explanation of these platforms, I try to explain the reasons why they are so popular, their most basic service or function, some of their additional services and functions, and how you can use them for your business. (I'm not suggesting that you use all four of these platforms. I hope you will read this section to understand the basics of each, and then decide whether you think they can help you meet your goals.)

Facebook for Business

(www.facebook.com)

Since Facebook is the 800-pound gorilla of the social web, I thought it would be best to start with it. Facebook has nearly a billion registered users at the time I'm writing this. I'm going to guess that you're one of them. Maybe you use it a lot, maybe you use it a little, or perhaps you've never used it before. But unless you live in a very remote part of the world, I'm sure you've heard about it. It's hard to walk outside of your home and not see the Facebook logo within a short radius. I see a Facebook logo more often than I see a Coca-Cola one. So, what is it that makes Facebook such a big deal? Simple: it's where the people are. Your friends, your neighbors, your aunts, your uncles, your cousins and probably your customers are on Facebook.

The ingeniousness of Facebook is that it's extremely easy to start using, not to mention free. In a matter of minutes you can have an account that's connected to a few of your close friends and family members. You will then see a "news feed," which is simply some information the people to whom you are connected have posted. It might be text, photos, video, or a combination of these. You then have the opportunity to click "like" or leave a comment. You may also see other comments people have written about that particular post. Of course, you can also make a post yourself, which will be seen by the people with whom you have decided to be connected. They then can "like" it or comment on it.

Although there is much more to Facebook than I have described here, that is the essence of what it does. It creates an easy (and free) way for people to communicate and share with each other.

How do you use Facebook as a business?

The basic way to use Facebook as a business is to have a Facebook "page" for your business. Having a page is different from having an account. When people use Facebook for personal use, they simply have an account. This account has various features, including the news feed. As a business, you need to create a page. Think of it like an interactive bulletin board. You can post pictures, videos, and text that you'd like people to see. You can post specials and promotions like "Next Thursday get 20% off if you wear a funny hat!" In essence, it's your website on Facebook. There are many ways you can customize it, but you need to do so within the structure that Facebook provides. That structure is versatile. You can have various tabs that have different types of information. You can even sell products on your Facebook page.

> *Side-note fact:* Facebook also offers opportunities for PPC display advertising (see below).

How do connections get made, and how do you build an audience?

For personal accounts to be connected, it starts with one person sending a "friend request" to another. The other person simply chooses whether or not to accept it. After a mutual connection is made, whenever one person posts something the other will see the post in their news feed. Besides connecting with individual people, you can also join groups. There are groups for almost any type of interest you can imagine. Some are public and open for anyone to join, while some are private and require the permission of the group administrator. You can also decide to start your own group.

For business accounts, it's different. Since businesses are eager to build as large of an audience as possible, they would send friend requests to everyone if they could. This would create a system full of spammy friend requests and make Facebook unpleasant for everyone. So, the way businesses can be connected with people (thereby creating an audience) is for people to click the "like" button on a business' Facebook page. Once someone does that, any information the business posts will show up in that person's news feed. (Have you ever seen ads that say "Like our Facebook page"? Now you know why.) This allows businesses to post information to a person's news feed. Imagine if hundreds, or thousands of people clicked "like" on your Facebook page. You can inform them about special discounts, remind them of your great products and services, or simply just say "Hello… Have a great day," all for free. If you want to see examples of how businesses use this method, search Facebook to find the page of a brand you know (such as Nike, Starbucks, or Home Depot). Click the "like" button. Then watch your news feed for messages from those companies. You'll get the idea of how this can be used and how effective it can be for keeping your business on people's minds.

Creating a Facebook Page

Creating a Facebook Page for your business is free and easy. You will first want to create a personal account. Although it's possible to set up a business account without setting up a personal profile, there are certain limitations that apply in that situation. It's usually better to set up a personal profile first, even if you don't plan to use it. Once you've setup a personal profile, follow these basic steps for creating a page:

1. Log in to your account.

2. From your profile page, click the "Pages" header in the navigation on the left. Then click "Create A Page."

3. Choose from the category options. These options let you define what kind of page you are creating. For example, you can create pages for local businesses, organizations, communities, special causes, brands, and more.

4. Name your page. The name of your page will be whatever you put in the box just under the category menu. Consider this carefully because it will be noticed by the search engines, as well as Facebook's own search function.

5. Add a profile picture for your business. This is the picture that will appear next to the posts your business puts on the page. The size should be 180 pixels by 180 pixels ideally.

6. Add information for the "About Page." This is where you can add descriptions and information about your business.

7. Add a cover photo. Your cover photo is large. It should ideally be 851 pixels wide by 315 pixels long. One rule Facebook has regarding the cover photo is that it must be mostly visual, as opposed to being filled with text. The rule states that the amount of text cannot exceed 20% of the photo area.

8. Set your permissions. Click "Edit Page," then "Manage Permissions" from the admin panel. There you can adjust various settings. By default, the settings allow people to send messages to your page. This is one feature you can decide to turn off. If you leave it on, be sure to check for messages regularly.

9. Start posting! Even if you don't have any "likes" yet, you will want to have a backlog of posts so that when people view your page, they can see the kinds of posts you will be making.

Remember that the main purpose of your Facebook page is to engage with your customers and contacts. Anyone who "likes" your page will receive your posts in their news feed. Before you post anything, be sure to check which mode you are in. There is a setting that switches the entity from which you are posting. You will see different settings, such as "Post as me" or "Post as ___ (your business)." Also, be sure to keep your posts on the light and fun side. Constantly trying to sell and promote is a mistake on Facebook. This can turn people off and cause them to "unlike" your page, meaning they won't receive your posts anymore. Also, it is a good idea to suggest good content. If you find an article you think people will be interested in, post a link to it. If you've added a new page to your website that explains something, let people know and post a link to that too.

> *Side-note fact*: Facebook allows for your page to have a custom URL, such as: www.facebook.com/your-custom-url-here/. This makes it easier to direct people to your Facebook page and gives SEO value as well.

Facebook's paid-advertising options

Facebook also offers the opportunity for paid advertisements. Facebook's pay-per-click display ad platform allows ads to appear on the side of the page as people look at their news feeds. A great feature of this platform is that you can target an audience based on specific interests, ages, and demographics. Another type of paid-advertising Facebook offers is called "Promoted Posts." Promoted Posts are posts that are put in a highly visible position so that the people who "like" your page will see them the next time they look at their news feed. They can also be expanded to be displayed to the friends of the people who like your page.

Other features of Facebook

- **Sponsored stories.** Sponsored stories are messages coming from friends about their engagement with a page that a business has paid to highlight, so there is a better chance people see them.

- **Contests and sweepstakes.** You can run contests in which the people who "like" your Facebook page can be eligible for a prize.

- **Fan Badge.** Facebook offers ways to promote your Facebook page on other websites, including your own, buy giving you a fan badge.

- **Facebook Insights.** Facebook Insights provides measurements on your page's performance, including how many people are seeing and responding to your posts.

- **Lists.** You can create custom lists of friends.

Top things to remember about Facebook

- Facebook is where the people are. It has more users than any other social network by far.

- The appeal of Facebook is that it is free and easy to use for sharing information with the people with whom we want to be connected.

- If you are a business, Facebook allows you to create a page for your business (also free). If people go to your page and click the "like" button, they will receive the posts from your business directly into their news feeds. Getting more "likes" from the right people is your main goal in order to keep your business visible.

- Your business' Facebook page is like an interactive bulletin board. You post information and the viewers can comment. It is a great way to engage with, and stay on the minds of your customers.

- Facebook also has a pay-per-click display ad platform that provides a wide array of targeting options, such as by location, interest, gender, age and other demographics.

- Facebook has a "Promoted Posts" feature which allows you to make a post that will be prominently displayed to all of the people who have "liked" your page, and possibly all of their friends.

- Facebook is not a place to do aggressive selling. It is a place to have a light, fun, and continuous rapport with people.

Twitter for Business

(www.twitter.com)

Twitter, another enormous social web platform, has become a part of everyday life for hundreds of millions of people. It's something we hear about all the time. Even the television newscasts are constantly referring to Twitter and the "tweets" of prominent people around the world. For those outside the Twitter universe, it can be a bit mysterious as to why it is such an important thing. After all, why do we need Twitter? Facebook is where the most of the people are. And what is the point of tweeting several times a day, like many people do? Do I really have to do this for my business?

The answer is no, you don't have to do it for your business. But it represents another opportunity on the web to help grow it. While Facebook is more about having mutual connections, Twitter is more like broadcasting. You follow someone on Twitter, as you might listen to a particular radio program. Just because you pay attention to what they say doesn't mean they are paying attention to what you say. Twitter is about sharing information to whoever wants to pay attention. You choose who you want to follow, and other Twitter users do the same. Another way to describe using Twitter is "micro-blogging." Just as blogging is about posting information for anyone who wants to see it,

Twitter is about posting information in the same manner—albeit in very small bites. (The maximum length of a tweet is 140 characters.)

So, what's the point of sending out tweets for public consumption? The point is to offer some interesting, useful or amusing pieces of information that people will enjoy; to take part in the conversation of the web; and (in the process) to gain positive recognition for the expertise, products or services that you offer. Once you have a few followers, you have the opportunity to do some effective and free promotion. This might seem like small potatoes, but don't underestimate it. The power of Twitter is immense. Here is an example of that power:

1. Let's say you own a flower shop. You sign up for a Twitter account. You put a link on your website that says, "Follow us on Twitter." And after a few weeks, you end up with four followers.

2. You make a dazzling flower arrangement for someone's wedding and decide to snap a photo of it to share with your four Twitter followers.

3. One of your four followers likes the photo so much that they forward it (or re-tweet it) to their followers—of which there are 39.

4. One of those 39 followers likes it so much that they re-tweet it to their followers—of which there are 153.

5. One of those 153 followers likes it so much that they re-tweet it to their followers—of which there are 4,890.

(And on, and on, and on.)

So, by you tweeting a great photo to your four followers, it could spread and be seen by thousands of people in a few short minutes or hours. Many of those people who see your photo might now decide to follow you also, which will increase the number of people who get your tweets directly. To put it simply, Twitter is VIRAL. Messages and information can spread extremely quickly and easily to large numbers of people. If you happen to witness a major news event and tweet about it immediately, it's possible that your tweet could be seen by millions of people in a short time span.

Although there is a lot more to Twitter than I just described, that explains its essence. It gives you a free and easy way to broadcast messages. And, needless to say, that could be very beneficial to most businesses.

> *Side-note fact*: On Facebook, an account is supposed to be based on a real identity/person. On Twitter, it doesn't work that way. Twitter allows you to simply choose a username and start tweeting. Twitter also allows you to have more than one account, unlike Facebook.

How easy is it to harness Twitter's power for your business?

In one sense, it's easy. All you need to do is sign up for a Twitter account, promote your account to your customers, and start tweeting messages (of 140 characters or fewer). In another sense, it's not easy at all. Succeeding with Twitter is mostly about two things: quantity of tweets and quality of tweets. Tweeting regularly is highly recommended. Once a day is okay. Four or five times a day is better. Most successful Twitter-users tweet multiple times per day. Does that sound like something you would like to do every day from now on?

Providing a regular stream of tweets every day is a challenging task to keep up, week-after-week, month-after-month, and year-after-year. It's a process of building followers who think you have something good to offer them regularly. Of course, the quality matters, too. Yes, a great tweet can go viral, but that's easier said than done. It takes something very interesting, funny, newsworthy, shocking, or educational to spread to large numbers of people. The best approach is to be genuine, consistent and realistic. Choose a strategy and routine that fits with your personality and lifestyle. Learning to enjoy it will go a long way in helping you succeed as well.

Types of messages on Twitter

Besides the standard tweet, there are different ways and formats for communicating on Twitter. Here are the five types of messages:

- Standard tweet

- Reply—a reply to someone else's tweet.

- Mention—a message that mentions the Twitter name of another user.

- Direct Message—a message you send privately to another Twitter user.

- Re-tweet—this is when you forward a tweet by someone else to your followers.

Using hashtags

The hashtag sign (#) serves a useful purpose on Twitter. Interestingly, it started from Twitter users and not Twitter itself. When you put a hashtag in front of a word or phrase, it marks that word or phrase as a keyword. It's like saying, "This is what the subject of the tweet is." That flags the tweet to show up when someone searches Twitter for that keyword. Twitter has a powerful search engine for finding tweets about various topics. For example, if you have #multi-vitamins in your tweet, and then someone searches #multi-vitamins on Twitter, your tweet can show up in the search results.

To use hashtags, remember a few important things. One: capitalization doesn't matter. The terms #BabyFood and #babyfood will bring the same result. Two: if your keyword is a phrase, there can be no spaces between the words. If the keyword you want to mark is hotels near Walt Disney World you would hashtag it as #hotelsnearwaltdisneyworld. Three: common etiquette dictates that you not use more than two hashtags per tweet. Adding more than two hashtags makes your tweets a bit too spammy for most people. It's good to mark keywords to be found in searches, but don't overdo it.

When you see hashtagged items in other people's tweets, clicking on them will send you to a search results page, where you'll find other tweets containing that hashtag. Near the top of the page you may click "Top," which will show you the tweets that have been re-tweeted the most times. You could also click "All," (which will show you all tweets that include that hashtag) or "People You Follow" (which will show you only the tweets of the people you follow who have used that hashtag).

Twitter's paid-advertising options

Twitter has some interesting paid-advertising options. I mentioned them in Part 3 of this book, but here is a brief recap:

> "Promoted Tweets" – This is where you create a tweet and set it to be seen at the top of your follower's timelines. You will then be charged if one of your followers clicks to take one of the following actions: re-tweet, reply, add to favorites, or clicks to see your profile. You may target promoted tweets to occur within a specified geographic area, by a particular device, by interests, by gender, or by similarity to existing followers.
>
> "Promoted Accounts" – The Promoted Accounts feature is intended to help you increase your follower-count. This will cause your account to be prominently displayed in the *Who to Follow* section of the Twitter page. You are charged only when a user follows you. Like Promoted Tweets, you can target Promoted Accounts to occur within a specified geographic area, by a particular device, by interests, by gender, or by similarity to existing followers.

Top things to remember about Twitter

- On Facebook, an account is supposed to be based on a real identity/person. On Twitter, it doesn't work that way. Twitter allows you to simply choose a username and start tweeting. Twitter also allows you to have more than one account, unlike Facebook.

- Using Twitter is like broadcasting on your own information channel. People may choose to follow you, or you may choose to follow them. It's not a mutual connection like being friends on Facebook.

- The power of Twitter is in how quickly and immensely viral it can be. A good tweet may be spread from your followers to their followers, and so on, with the possibility of it being seen by millions of people.

- Using Twitter is sometimes called "micro-blogging" because you are distributing information in very small bites (up to 140 characters).

- Hashtags (#) are used to denote keywords in your tweets. They are valuable because they can make your tweets visible when people search Twitter for the subjects to which your keywords refer.

- Twitter can be valuable for your business because it can make people aware of your expertise, products or services.

- Although the rewards may be substantial, it takes a continuous effort to succeed on Twitter. The most important things are the quantity and quality of the tweets.

- Twitter offers paid-advertising options known as "Promoted Tweets" and "Promoted Accounts".

LinkedIn

(www.linkedin.com)

LinkedIn is another massively popular social web platform. It has similarities to other social platforms, but some key differences as well. The primary difference is that it's centered on people's jobs, careers and businesses. It's the go-to place for displaying your achievements and business credentials. It's a place to connect with others who share similar interests or have similar goals. And it's a place where many companies go to look for new employees and freelance contractors to hire. LinkedIn is free to use, although there are premium memberships available which allow more features and freedoms for making connections.

Although LinkedIn has many great features, its most basic function is that of an online resume. When you create an account on LinkedIn, you are prompted to complete a profile that represents what you have to offer in the workplace. When you create your profile, you put your best foot forward to explain your skills, specialties, achievements, education, and career experience. Profiles are very important and should be made as clear and complete as possible. This is how other members of LinkedIn will view you and decide if you are worth seeking out for a connection.

Since LinkedIn is geared toward careers and business, it requires a much different approach than Facebook. On LinkedIn, the objective is to obtain credibility and respect in your profession. You want to present yourself in a professional manner. To help build credibility among your network of contacts on LinkedIn, you have the opportunity to request recommendations from people who know you. You may also garner "endorsements" from others members who are inclined to vouch for you in that way.

Another important feature of LinkedIn is its groups. There are groups that can be a fantastic source of information and exposure for the members. Members post questions about topics related to the group, and other members attempt to provide answers. This creates a healthy learning and networking opportunity. It also gives the members a chance to shine by displaying their knowledge to the group, which can lead to more connections and endorsements.

Methods of contacting others

For the people who are your 1st degree (direct) connections, you are free to contact them directly by clicking the "send email" button on their profile pages. Contacting 2nd- and 3rd- degree people involves using a feature called "Introductions." When you open a new account, LinkedIn provides you with five introductions for free. To have the ability to send more, you need to upgrade to a premium account. This is how introductions work: Find a 1st- degree connection who is connected to the person to whom you want the introduction to go. Send an introduction message to your 1st- degree connection and ask that he or she forward it to the person to whom you want the introduction to go. (Of course, your direct connection has the option of declining your request.) If it does get forwarded, the person who receives it gets the option of accepting or declining the introduction. If the introduction is accepted, that doesn't make you 1st- degree connections. An invitation still must to be sent for that to occur, which would require getting an email address for the person.

LinkedIn also offers messaging capabilities called InMail and Openlink, but these are only available to premium members. InMail allows you to directly contact anyone on the LinkedIn network without an introduction. OpenLink allows you to receive OpenLink messages from anyone on the LinkedIn network. With OpenLink, you can keep your email address private while opening yourself up to more contacts and connection possibilities.

Contacts & connections

Network building on LinkedIn involves your contacts and connections. A contact is someone of whom you are aware, but is not part of your network. It might be someone you found while doing a search. It might be someone you already have as a Gmail, AOL, Hotmail or Outlook email contact. Or, it might be someone who's connected to one or your connections. To turn a contact into a connection, you send the contact an invitation to connect. If they accept your invitation, you are then connected as 1st- degree connections.

Since LinkedIn is your network of professionals online, it is vital to keep your reputation in mind. The goal is to build connections and credibility. Therefore, it's important to be cautious about your 1st-degree connections. The more you know about the people you invite (or who invite you), the better. When you receive an invitation, ask yourself, *"Does this person seem like someone who would have a positive effect on my network, and perhaps give me a positive recommendation?"* Also, someone who is your 1st-degree connection has the ability to access all of your connections. Consider how that might reflect on you. Your reputation on LinkedIn should be guarded carefully, so it's not a good idea to send or accept invitations without some degree of caution.

Would LinkedIn be helpful for your business?

The three main benefits of using LinkedIn are: finding people with whom to connect, being found by others, and keeping in touch with your connections. Obviously, each of these benefits can have tremendous value in the business world. As a business owner, you need to decide if this type of networking is right for you. As with other social web platforms, it takes a continuous effort to reap the benefits. It's not something you can set and forget. You have to spend time on a regular basis cultivating real, human connections and interactions. It is an investment of time, but the possible rewards can be substantial as your LinkedIn presence grows steadily over time

Setting up your profile

As I mentioned earlier, your profile acts as your online resume on LinkedIn. It is important because it is how other members will get a first impression of you. Based on your profile, they will decide if they think you are worth connecting with. You should strive to complete your profile in the best way you can. Here are some tips for creating a good profile:

- Be sure to include your picture.
- Be sure to include your contact information.
- Mention if you are freelance/independent in your line of work.
- Put your skills in the Professional Headline. Your name and professional headline are the only things that appear in search results on LinkedIn.
- Write a good background description of yourself, but not too long. Two paragraphs is a good length.
- List languages you speak and how well you speak them.

How to create a company page

Creating a company page on LinkedIn is a free and simple process. One important caveat is that it is required to have an email address that is on its own distinct domain. That means it needs to be like "pete@petescompany.com," and can't be a Gmail, Hotmail, AOL, or other common email domain.

When you have a company page, other LinkedIn members can choose to follow your company, much as they do on Twitter or by "liking" your Facebook page. You can then post status updates to inform your followers of new products, services, promotions, or anything else about your business that they might be interested in.

To create a company page:

1. At the top of your LinkedIn homepage, go to Interests, and then Companies.

2. Click "Add a Company" on the upper right area of the page.
3. Enter the name of the company and your work email address.
4. Click "Continue" and follow the instructions for confirming your work email address.
5. Add information about your company.

Paid-advertising on LinkedIn

LinkedIn has its own pay-per-click ad system for reaching out to other members. The ads can appear in two different places: on the sidebar, and at the top of the site. They include a photo, 25-character headline, and 75-character description. You can target your ads by industry, job function, groups, geography, age and more. You can also split-test ads to see which get a better response.

Top things to remember about LinkedIn

- The most basic function of LinkedIn is to act as your online resume.
- People search LinkedIn to find workers and businesses that offer certain skills. Your Profile is what they will look at to decide if they want to do business with you or connect with you.
- The objective on LinkedIn is to build credibility for yourself and/or your business. Features like recommendations and endorsements help in that way.
- LinkedIn has many groups based around certain topics. Getting involved in those groups (by asking and answering questions) is a great way to get information and display your expertise on a subject, which can lead to new connections.
- Emails are sent to create connections. Your 1st-degree connections are the people who you can contact directly. Your 2nd-degree connections are the connections of your first-degree connections (and so on.)
- Contacting 2nd- and 3rd-degree people involves using a feature called Introductions.
- LinkedIn is free, but you may upgrade to a premium account.

- With a free account, you are given five introductions to use.

- Premium accounts allow you more freedoms for contacting people outside of your 1st-degree connections.

- It's very important to complete your profile as much as possible.

- You may create a company page for your business that others can follow.

- LinkedIn has paid-advertising options that give you more exposure to other members.

Google+ for Business

(plus.google.com)

Another major social web platform is Google Plus (or Google +). Google+ came on the scene in 2011 and has tried to emulate Facebook in a number of ways. Facebook and Google+ work similarly, in that they are a means of easily connecting with the people in our lives. They both have a prominent viewing area for viewing posts. (On Facebook, it's called the news feed. On Google+ it's called the stream.) Like Facebook, Google+ is also free.

Probably the biggest difference between Facebook and Google+ is that when you have a new connection on Facebook, it goes into a general list of friends by default. On Google+, the people you are connected to go into your "circles." You may have numerous circles that relate to different areas of your life. For example, you can have different circles for your family members, classmates, and business associates, and yet another for your friends. You could create one called "Golf Buddies" that's only for the people with whom you play golf. Facebook lets you do this also (by creating lists), but in Google+ it is built right into the system. You add people by clicking "Add to Your Circles." Keeping connections in different circles is very useful, since it allows you to send posts that relate to those people, without having to send it to everyone else with whom you are connected. For example, if there was a family reunion coming up in your family, you might want to post something about it to the circle of your family members. If there was something going on at work, you could post about it only to the circle of your work associates.

Also like Facebook, Google+ allows you to create a page for your business. This page is like an interactive bulletin board that allows you to post many types of information, including written posts, photos, videos, links, and combinations of these. The people who decide to "+1" your page will receive your posts in their stream.

Should you use Google+ for your business? And why?

Since Facebook is a similar platform with many more users, why should a business spend time using Google+? Isn't it redundant if you're already using Facebook? Yes, Facebook is a similar platform with many more users. And yes, it is a bit redundant to be using Google+ while you are also using Facebook. There are some very nice features on Google+, and there are hundreds of millions of people using it. But the biggest reason that businesses keep a presence on Google+ is *simply because it's Google*. Undoubtedly, Google is the king of search engines. Consumers worldwide are using Google to find the products, services, and information they want. As business owners, we want to be as visible as possible to the people searching for the products or services we offer. Google+ pages allow our businesses to have a place that shows we are a credible business that engages with the public. This can help with our rankings in Google searches. Also, "Google+ Local Pages" is Google's new directory of local businesses. It is now intertwined with their older system called "Google Places."

When it comes to Google+, one of the best sayings going around is, "If you care about Google, you care about Google+." I think that sums it up. Besides the fact that Google+ is an excellent social platform with many great features, it represents an opportunity to help our businesses become more credible with the Google search engine. Also, keep in mind that Google is the owner of YouTube, another powerhouse in the area of Internet marketing. There are some nice ways that your Google+ and YouTube accounts can work together to help your business. (See more about YouTube in Part 6 of this book.)

What's with the "+1"?

Both Facebook and Google+ allow individuals and businesses to post information for their friends or followers to see. They also allow businesses to create pages for interacting with the public. On Facebook, you have the option of clicking "like" under a post or on a business page. The "+1" on Google+ is more-or-less the same thing; you are expressing your approval of that particular post or page.

If you click the "+1" button on a Google+ business page, you will be given the option to add that business to one of your circles. That would mean that the posts of that business would flow into your stream for the circle you choose. On Facebook, clicking the "like" button on a business page will also open up your news feed to the posts of that business.

How to create a Google+ page for your business?

Google+ allows businesses and other organizations to create a page for posting information and engaging with the public. Here's how to create a page for your business:

1. In the left-side navigation of Google+, click "Pages"
2. Click "Create a Page."
3. Choose a category for your page. You will have several options, including Product, Company, Local Business, Entertainment, etc.
4. Click Finish.

After creating the page, try to add as much information as you can to inform the viewers of your page about your business.

If you want to change information in your page's profile at a later time, here's how to do it:

1. Make sure you're using Google+ as your page (and not as yourself).
2. Click "Profile" on the left.
3. Choose the section you wish to edit.
4. Click the save button when you are finished.

Other Features of Google+

Google+ has a great many features that you might want to test drive. Although some of them come and go as they test new functions, here are some of the mainstays:

- **Authorship.** If you create original content on your blog, Google gives you the opportunity to create a visual connection between you and the content you publish. It will enhance your visibility in the search results. When you claim your Authorship, your Google+ profile picture will show up next to your posts in the search results pages.

- **Hangouts.** Google+ Hangouts are a way to connect visually with up to ten people at the same time through the Hangouts interface. There are many uses for Hangouts, including hosting live Q & A with your customers. You can also record the Hangout and use YouTube to make the video available to anyone.

- **Badge.** The Google+ badge allows you to link your website to your Google+ page.

- **Events.** Through Google+, you can host events that allow you to build and send invitations to the circles of people you want to invite.

- **Hashtags.** Just like with Twitter, hashtags (#) denote keywords in your posts. If you don't put hashtags in your posts, Google+ sometimes might suggest hashtags for you to use. Clicking on a hashtagged item will show content that relates to that keyword.

- **Communities.** With a large variety of communities for different topics and interests, Google+ provides this great way of connecting with others. You can also create your own community.

- **Chats.** To start a chat with someone, navigate to their profile and click the Hangout icon.

Top things to know about Google+

- Google+ is Google's social web platform. It is similar to Facebook for making connections with the people in your life, and it allows you to create a page for your business.

- One of the main differentiating features of Google+ from Facebook is that Google+ has you add new people to your "circles." Circles are a way to keep groups separated, such as family members and old classmates. When you make a post, you may choose one or more circles to receive it.

- As with the other social web platforms, the key to reaping benefits is to post often and engage with others.

- The homepage of your Google+ account shows the posts of the people, businesses and organizations with whom you are connected in your circles. This part of your homepage is called the stream. (It's similar to the news feed on Facebook.)

- One of the main reasons businesses use Google+ is to help build credibility with the Google search engine, which will hopefully lead to higher rankings in the search results.

- Google+ Local Pages is Google's new directory of local businesses. It is now intertwined with their older platform called Google Places.

- When you click the "+1" button on a page or post, you are essentially expressing your praise or approval.

- Google+ has many great features including communities, hangouts, event-hosting, and authorship for original content you create.

Summary

Most important things to know from this section

- The biggest change on the web in the last several years is the enormous growth of social websites.

- Social sites offer the possibility of reaching a large audience for little or no cost.

- The key to success on the social web is active engagement. There is no way around it. The amount of time you want to invest is up to you, but it needs to be on continuous basis.

- The social web is not a place for hard selling. It's a place to have a positive and friendly rapport with people.

- Facebook is the largest social network. It allows your business to have a page for showing information and posts to those who have "liked" your page. It also has paid-advertising options.

- Twitter is an extremely popular platform that involves writing short messages (called tweets) that go out to anyone who decides to be your follower. It is an extremely viral platform. Part of the custom on Twitter is to re-tweet messages that are especially good, funny, or interesting. Twitter also has paid-advertising options.

- LinkedIn is the social web platform for businesses and professionals. The most basic function of LinkedIn is to act as your online resume. It provides ways for you to network with other people and build a credible reputation by obtaining recommendations and endorsements. It also allows you to build a company page, and use PPC display advertising for exposure on the network.

- Google+ has many similarities to Facebook. A key feature of Google+ is "circles." Circles are a way of categorizing your connections into groups that are similar, such as family members or work associates. Part of the appeal of Google+ is to gain favor with the Google search engine, and (hopefully) be more visible in Google search results.

- Google+ Local Pages is now Google's directory of local businesses. It is now intertwined with their older platform, Google Places.

Most important things to do

- Prioritize. If you want to invest time with the social web, choose your strategy and priorities carefully. A lot of time needs to be spent in the pursuit of followers, "likes," "+1's," etc. There is endless possibility out there, so it's important to choose your priorities.

- Engage. There is no great way to automate or "fake" a presence on the social web. Hiring someone to do it for you can give you more exposure and possibly help your business, but the real advantage is when people get a sense of who you are over time.

- Budget. Think about how much time you want to invest and stick to a routine. Make sure you stay focused on your goals and don't get too distracted. It's like going to a party for business: it's better if you enjoy yourself, but don't forget why you are there.

- Commit. Reaping the benefits of the social web doesn't usually come quickly. It can be a very slow-build proposition. Commit to doing it for the long-haul (i.e., over a period of years). A few weeks or a few months of engagement is not enough.

- Set goals that are specific and attainable, such as to have 20 "likes" on your Facebook page, or 20 Twitter followers.

Most important things NOT to do

- Try to build up a following too quickly. It's a marathon, not a sprint.

- Be phony or insincere. Just as in other social situations, it's good to simply be yourself. You will have more success that way in gaining connections than by trying to be something or someone you are not.

- Ignore your friends and followers. Always spend some time reading and commenting on the posts of others.

- Over-promote your business. The goal of the social web is to give you exposure and help you make connections. That in turn will help you get customers. Build up your credibility with people before promoting what your business has to offer. Trying too hard to sell will be an immediate turn-off.

- Be too business-like. Keep your posts on the light side usually. Show some humor and personality.

Part 6-YouTube, Email Marketing, Podcasting, & Craigslist

In this section, I will explain several major opportunities the Internet has to offer. Each of these methods has immense power and can bring an enormous amount of visibility to your business. They are all free or low-cost methods, and have been known to bring great ROI. They are: YouTube, email marketing, podcasting, and Craigslist.

YouTube

(www.youtube.com)

YouTube was founded in 2005 by three employees of PayPal. In 2006, it was bought by Google for 1.6 billion dollars. Since its simple and humble beginnings, YouTube has become the dominant behemoth of the online video world. It has a staggering amount of web traffic, including more than one billion unique users each month, more than four billion video views each day, and over one trillion video views since its inception.

How can YouTube's explosive growth be explained? Several factors play a part. Before YouTube, there was no centralized place or standard format for web video. Although web video existed, there were different technologies that made it work (which is still true today). This means that if a video appeared on a particular web page, it was only possible to play it if you had the proper plug-in software. Back then, there were more compatibility issues. The guys who started YouTube had the idea of creating a site that would convert all videos to just one format, Flash, that had the broadest compatibility. Since YouTube was able to convert videos to the broadest compatibility format, it became the most popular site for uploading videos. Besides solving a compatibility issue, YouTube also created an easy-to-use interface and elements of a friendly community. Viewers of videos are often able to write text comments, create video comments, and give ratings to videos.

Is YouTube good for businesses? You better believe it. Many millionaires have been made by using YouTube's awesome power. Why is YouTube so good for business? Because of the huge number of people who are exposed to it. People go to YouTube for entertainment, but they also go for educational purposes. Instructional videos are very popular. If there is something you are qualified to teach, you can upload a video of a lesson and then use it to generate traffic to your website. Another key benefit of uploading YouTube videos is that they show up in Google searches (remember who owns YouTube?). For example, if you're a CPA and make videos about how to fill in certain tax forms, your video can show up in the search results whenever someone searches the phrase "how to fill out a W-9 form." That video can act as a free commercial for your services and help drive traffic to your website.

Would it be beneficial to use YouTube for your business?

The answer is probably a resounding "yes." Of course, I don't know what your business is, but the simple fact that you're reading this book tells me you are interested in greater visibility on the Internet. YouTube offers that opportunity in spades and without the time investment that the social web platforms demand. By uploading videos to YouTube and tagging them with keywords, the videos can do a lot of work for you without requiring that you spend time on them on a daily or weekly basis. Of course, engaging with others in the community can be beneficial, but it's not a necessity as it is with Facebook, Twitter, LinkedIn, and Google+. My advice is to take advantage of the free visibility from YouTube as soon as possible.

How to make videos

These days, equipment for making videos is not hard to come by. Video cameras are inexpensive and easy to use. There's a good chance you have a video camera in one of your electronic devices, such as your laptop, tablet computer, or smartphone. It's also easy to find video editing software. If you have an Apple or Windows computer made in the last eight years, you have software for editing. On Apple computers the software is called iMovie, and on Windows it's called Windows Movie Maker.

Here are some tips for recording and editing your videos:

- Good lighting is very important for video. Use daylight if you can, otherwise make sure the room you are in is as well-lit as possible.

- Make sure the camera is as steady as possible. Video with a lot of shaking is not very pleasant to watch. Consider using a tripod or something else to mount the camera.

- If you have zoom control, don't use it much. It's better to keep the frame steady and avoid zooming.

- Music helps! A little music can add life to a video. In your editing software, you will have the ability to add a music track. (You must have the legal right to use recordings of music. If you search the web for "royalty free music," you will find recordings that you can purchase the rights to use.)

- Add titles. Adding titles means adding words to the video that can be read. You will find this capability in your editing software.

- Plan your video carefully. It's easier to make videos if you have some pre-planned "edit points." That way you can record the video in smaller pieces and then put them together.

- Audio is very important. Make sure the words of people speaking can be heard clearly. Unless you have an external microphone, it helps if the person speaking is not far from the recording device. Avoid excessive wind or crowd noise.

Ideas for your video content

What will your video be about? You want it to be useful to the viewer and a good promotional vehicle for your business. It doesn't need to be long—two or three minutes can be enough. Here are some ideas to get you thinking:

- Teach something people can learn.

- Make videos that log activity with your business, such as current projects.

- Interview an expert or have someone interview you.

- Use photographs to make a slide-show video. Then add music and a voiceover.

- Funny videos are popular on YouTube. Can you think of a way to show something funny that's related to your business?

- Answer customer FAQs.

- Explain a future project your business is working on.

- Introduce your co-workers.

- Make a video of testimonials from your customers.

How to upload and optimize your videos

Here's how to upload and optimize a video on YouTube:

- Log in to your YouTube account (if you don't have one, you can create one for free).

- Click the "Upload" button in the top right corner.

- Add a title to your video.

- Add a description of your video.

- Add tags for your video.

The title, description, and tags are very important because they are what will help your video be found by people searching YouTube—or Google, for that matter. Think carefully about the words you choose, especially for the tags. You also have a variety of options you can set for each video, such as the thumbnail image that will represent your video, privacy settings (public, private, or unlisted), category, whether to allow comments from viewers, whether to allow others to embed the video on their web pages, and more.

Ways to promote your videos

Whenever you upload a new video to your YouTube account, it's always a good idea to promote it. Here are a few ways to promote your videos:

- Embed your video in a blog post.

- Embed the video in your Facebook page or a Facebook post.
- Tweet a link to your video.
- Embed the video on your website.
- Announce it in your Google+ circles.
- Link to it from your LinkedIn profile or company page.

Important and useful features of YouTube

Channels. A YouTube channel is the home page of an account. It shows the videos that have been uploaded and other information that can be entered. Channels can be customized to create a certain look, such as changing the color scheme and background.

Subscriptions. People can click a button to subscribe to your YouTube channel. If they do, they will be notified of any new videos you upload.

Annotations. Annotations allow you to create clickable links in your videos. They can link to other videos, your Google+ account, or to a "subscribe" button. This can be used for a call-to-action.

Analytics. YouTube provides extensive analytics information about your videos views, traffic sources, demographic data, geographic data, and much more.

Captions and subtitles. These make your videos more accessible to those who are deaf or hard of hearing, or to those who speak another language.

Google+ integration. You can directly connect your YouTube account with your Google+ pages and posts.

Google+ Hangouts. If you use "Hangouts On Air" on Google+, you can use YouTube to show the video to more people.

Paid-advertising opportunities. Through Google AdWords, you can access a variety of paid-advertising options for reaching YouTube's massive audience.

Top things to know about YouTube

- YouTube is the king of video on the Internet. It has a staggering amount of traffic, and is the second most searched website in the world.

- YouTube presents a great opportunity for businesses to gain free exposure.

- Your YouTube videos can be great vehicles for driving traffic to your website.

- To get started with YouTube, you open an account (for free) and then upload your videos. You will give your videos a title, description, and tags so they will show up in searches for the keywords you've chosen.

- YouTube videos often show up in Google searches (YouTube is owned by Google).

- To record your videos, make sure to have good lighting. Also, avoid camera shaking and zooming.

- There are many types of videos you can make, such as instructional, humorous, or ones that include interviews or testimonials.

- Through Google AdWords, you can use YouTube's paid-advertising options to reach a large audience.

Email Marketing

Email marketing is one of the most effective marketing methods in existence. It doesn't take much time, doesn't cost much money (if any) and has been known to have greater conversion rates than many other types of marketing. To best explain what email marketing is, I will first explain what it isn't. Email marketing is not creating, buying, or renting a list of email addresses of people you do not know, only to send them emails about what you're selling. This might have been considered email marketing in 1996, but it's not anymore. As you might know, this practice is called "spamming," and it is illegal unless you follow some strict guidelines (see the legal guidelines at www.brickway.net/can-spam-act/). Another reason spamming is no longer considered email marketing is that it doesn't work. Internet service providers have become adept at filtering out spam. This means that most spam email will not even make it into the targeted person's inbox. Sure, some gets through (as most of us can attest), but the majority of it doesn't. Even if the email does get into someone's inbox, that person will most likely delete it faster than you can say "trash bin," and may even report you as a spammer (which can have serious consequences).

So, what does it take to do legitimate email marketing these days? In a word: permission. Most of us have certain brands, stores, and services that we like. We sometimes give permission for these businesses to contact us on a regular basis through email (or snail mail). How and when do we give that permission? We do it when we join their "rewards program," or some similar type of gimmick. We might sign up to get their emails because we actually want them. Most of the time, however, we're simply bribed into giving out our email addresses in order to receive discounts, free gifts, award points, or some other benefit.

Can email marketing help your business?

Most likely, the answer to this question is "yes." One of the great marketing minds of our time, Seth Godin, wrote that the Internet has brought us to a time where "permission marketing" rules the day. This means businesses need to have a patient and gradual approach to selling. Permission marketing involves seeking permission to market before actually trying to do it. The opposite of permission marketing (according to Seth) is "interruption marketing." Interruption marketing means trying to make sales and get conversions from strangers without any courtship, or "permission" to market to them first. For several decades, interruption marketing ruled the day. We bought products and services based on the ads we saw on TV, in the newspaper, in magazines, etc. Email and the social web have brought us to a time when real and personal connections are important to our buying decisions. For businesses to stay on people's minds today, it requires regular interaction that's friendly and not aggressive. Email marketing is a perfect vehicle for your business to do just that.

Interruption marketing still has a role to play in the marketplace. After all, how can a new business get noticed without using some traditional interruption tactics? Interruption marketing can start a relationship with a customer. Permission marketing, such as email marketing and the use of social platforms, should then be used to keep the relationship going.

How can your business start an email marketing campaign?

To have an email marketing strategy like I described above is not that difficult. There are several services available that can make the whole process easy. Here is a basic rundown of how it works:

1. Decide on a strategy for collecting email addresses from your customers and visitors to your website (such as an offer for a discount, or a free gift).

2. Sign up for an account with an email marketing service (for a list of services, go to www.brickway.net/email-marketing-services/).

3. Follow the instructions from the email marketing service for installing an opt-in form to your website.

4. As people opt-in, the email addresses will appear in your account with the email marketing service.

5. Send emails on a scheduled basis to keep your business fresh on the minds of the people on your list. The email marketing service will make that easy by offering you many options for how and when the emails should be sent, including various design templates you can choose to use.

Making your plan

An effective email marketing campaign starts with having a good plan. First, consider the most important questions: *What types of messages will be sent? What type of content will be included (e.g., tips or "how-to" advice)? How often will emails be sent?* As you make your plan, keep your most important goals in mind.

Once you have a general strategy, consider these questions as you go: *Do you have an appealing subject line? Do you have a have a clear call-to-action? Is your contact information easy to see? Do you have an "unsubscribe" button for them to opt-out if they desire? Are you including* links to your social web pages and videos? How does the email look on smartphone devices?

Another aspect to consider is how you will monitor the results. Through various email marketing services, you are able to see statistics, such as click-through-rates, unsubscribes, sharing rates, and more.

Types of emails you might send in your campaigns

You want your emails to be interesting and appealing to your readers. It's best to make them personable and informative. Adding a personal touch and useful information will help keep your business on their minds in a positive way. Be sure to mention any discounts or promotions you are running at that time as well. Here are some ideas for the content of your emails:

- Tell stories about things happening with your business.
- Offer tips or advice on topics related to your business.
- Tell stories about your workers or customers.
- Mention new products or services you will be offering soon.
- Write something to pique their curiosity, and then provide a link to a page on your website that has the "answer."

Top things to know about email marketing

- Email marketing is effective, easy and inexpensive (or free).
- Email marketing does not mean renting or buying a list of addresses only to spam them on a regular basis. It means building your own list of people who have agreed to receive your emails.
- Spamming is illegal, unless you follow the strict guidelines of the Can-Spam Act of 2003. (www.brickway.net/can-spam-act/)
- One of the best ways to build an email list is to offer something in exchange for signing up for your mailings, such as a discount or free gift.
- Spamming doesn't work due to modern email filters and the general distaste of the public for unsolicited mail.

- There are several email marketing services that make this very easy and almost fully automated. (www.brickway.net/email-marketing-services/)

- It's important to have an appealing subject line and a clear call-to-action.

- Adding a personal touch along with useful information will help keep your business on your readers' minds in a positive way.

Podcasting

It's hard to precisely explain what a podcast is, or what the origins of podcasting are. It can be related to different things from the past, including "audio blogging" which started in the 1980's. We can easily assume, however, that the term "podcast" is a combination of the words "iPod" and "broadcast." Podcasts are generally known to be audio recordings that have educational content, entertainment, or some other type of content and are usually disbursed in a series of episodes. (Think of the old-time radio shows that would broadcast new episodes every week. That's what most podcasts are like.)

Podcasts are a much more flexible format than perhaps any other type of broadcasting. Podcasts can have video as well as audio. They may include whatever content a person wishes to create, be whatever length a person wants them to be, and be released as often or as seldom as desired by the creator. In those ways, it really is similar to blogging. Blogging, however, tends to be driven more by written articles, while podcasting is driven more by audio and video.

A big part of the podcasting medium is the subscription. If people like your podcast and want to hear future episodes, they can subscribe. They will then receive your new episodes automatically in their podcast player (such as iTunes). For most podcasts, however, it's not necessary to get a subscription to listen. Episodes may be downloaded and listened to individually.

Could podcasting be good for your business?

Let me start by saying that this is a very powerful medium. Podcasts have become extremely popular in recent years, and are constantly gaining in popularity. There are many businesses that have flourished from the podcasts they have created. The public is always looking for fresh and interesting content. A podcast that has high-quality information, or is entertaining can get a massive amount of free exposure. There is practically no limit to the possibilities that can result from quality podcasts.

Whether podcasting is right for your business depends on your goals and abilities. Suppose you create a good podcast and build up a decent-sized audience over time. Would you be able to leverage that to promote your business? If you create a podcast called "Eating the Vegan Way," and have books, DVDs and other merchandise available for purchase on your website, your podcast could give a huge boost to your sales (assuming your merchandise is related to your podcast topic). Podcast listeners tend to give more time and attention than readers of blogs. This gives you the opportunity to establish yourself as an authority or thought-leader on a subject.

Ideas for your podcast

Your podcast can be any length you choose. There is no normal amount of time. A ten-minute podcast can be a popular and effective one. It's good to have a name, a format and a theme to be consistent about. Try to inform your listeners (or viewers) what they can expect from you, and when they can expect it. Here are a few types of content you might want to consider for your podcast:

- Instructional content, such as a series of lessons related to your business
- News about current events in your industry
- Discussions about current events in your industry
- Reviews and opinions about people or products in your industry
- Interviews with people related to your business

Technical aspects of podcasting

Like blogging, podcasting normally uses RSS feeds. (RSS stands for "Really Simple Syndication.") This allows your podcast to have subscribers. The RSS feed from your podcast alerts directories (such as iTunes, Stitcher and Zune) when you have a new episode available. Subscribers to the podcast will receive the new podcast in their podcast/media player. Before uploading each new podcast episode to a web server, you need to have these items prepared: title, host or talent name, podcast subtitle, description, and artwork design in the form of a square image.

Podcasting tools and services available

Here are some services that can ease the process of creating and hosting podcasts:

> www.spreaker.com
> www.buzzsprout.com
> www.podbean.com
> www.blogtalkradio.com
> www.mixlr.com

Top things to know about podcasting

- Podcasts can include audio and/or video, and are an immensely popular type of broadcasting.

- Podcasts are similar to blogs in some ways. They may include whatever type of content the owner wants to create, be whatever length the owner decides is appropriate, and be created at whatever time intervals the owner chooses.

- Podcasts have RSS feeds that allow people to subscribe and automatically receive new episodes in their podcast player (such as iTunes).

- Podcasting is a great way to establish yourself as an expert in your field.

- Podcasts can be a great vehicle for driving traffic to your website.

- There are various services available to greatly ease the process of creating and uploading podcasts.

Craigslist

(www.craigslist.com)

Craigslist began in 1995 when Craig Newmark decided to send a regular email to friends about events happening in San Francisco, California. The list was popular. More and more people wanted to receive it. In 1996, Craig decided to turn it into a website that allowed people to add their own listings. Craig was surprised when people started posting other types of listings besides events. The rest (as they say) is history. Craigslist is now one of the world's most-visited websites, and is the king of classified advertising on the web. Craigslist now has seven-hundred local sites in seventy countries, receiving over a hundred million new posts and around fifty billion page views every month.

Why is Craigslist so popular? The popularity of Craigslist can probably be explained by its ultra-simple interface, its variety of useful categories, and the fact that it's free to use.* Since it gets such an enormous amount of web traffic, you may easily post an ad that will be seen by lots of people quickly. It only takes a few minutes to create an ad. Then it takes roughly fifteen minutes for that ad to be live and viewable on the web. People can browse the categories on Craigslist to look at ads, or they might simply do a search for what they are looking for. They might search "leather sofa," "carpet cleaning service," or "three bedroom house." The results they see will be sorted by the date and time of the most recent postings. Although people use Craigslist for many different reasons, the three most popular reasons are: advertising goods and services, meeting people, and job hunting.

*Actually, Craigslist is not always free. They make their money by charging for posts in certain categories in certain areas, such as job postings in the San Francisco Bay area, brokered apartment rentals in New York City, and therapeutic services all around the United States.

Could Craigslist be helpful to your business?

There is no doubt that a lot of business is done through Craigslist. It serves a purpose that no other website serves at this time (factoring in its huge amount of traffic). If you think there is a chance you could find customers through Craigslist, you should try it. One of the great things about this outlet is that it's easy and painless to try. Perhaps do a few tests over a couple of weeks. Making it work for you might just be a matter of trial and error. If you decide to try it, here are some tips to help you succeed:

- Make your titles stand out.
- Add details so people can understand more about what you are offering.
- Add images to your ads.
- Use keywords in your titles and text to make your ads more likely to appear in searches.
- Start with a question, such as "Are you looking for an easier way to _____?"
- Make your ad relevant to the local community.
- Include a call-to-action.
- Instead of pushing for sales immediately, try to get a response for a free offer (like a free consultation).
- Keep your prices on the higher side so there is room for negotiation.
- Repost your ad after 48 hours.
- Create an account. If you create an account you can edit, repost, and delete more easily.
- Carefully consider the time that you post. Remember that posts appear in order of the date and time of posting.
- Craigslist allows you to use hyperlinks in your ads, which may be a helpful feature for viewers who want more information. To make a hyperlink in your ad, just type the web address starting with http:// and the system will automatically turn it into a hyperlink.

Playing by the rules

Just as on other areas of the web, there are always those who will go to obnoxious lengths to become more visible. Craigslist may seem like a big free-for-all, but there are rules. Without these rules, Craigslist would be so full of spammy posts that no one would bother using the service. The most important rule about using Craigslist has to do with the frequency and location of your ads. It reads as follows: You may post to one category and in one city no more than once every 48 hours. Craigslist ads show in the order of the most recent. For that reason, advertisers would love to be able to repost their ads more often than every 48 hours. That would give them more visibility near the top. Craigslist has filtering systems that detect when people break the rules. If their system detects that you are not abiding by the rules, it will take down your ads and might cancel your account.

Craigslist security and anonymity

Craigslist has a very good system for keeping your email address anonymous from the readers of your ads. It allows you to receive the response messages by email, but "anonymizes" your email address. This feature is called "Craigslist mail relay." It works two ways: protecting the advertiser and also protecting people who reply to ads. (Anonymized email is the default setting when you post an ad, but you may also choose to show your email address.)

Unlike Amazon and eBay, Craigslist has no rating system for members and sellers. Absolutely anyone can go to sell or buy. The fact that Craigslist allows us to be anonymous is both a good and bad thing. The good part is that it protects your identity from the public, rather than requiring you to display your name and contact information. The bad part is that it creates a platform for shadier characters to operate. Always be cautious when communicating on Craigslist. Examine all communications carefully while in the anonymous framework before giving anyone your full name or contact information.

Other classified ad sites

Although none of these come close to having the amount of traffic that Craigslist has, you might find one of these other classified sites to be helpful:

> www.usfreeads.com
> www.backpage.com
> www.yahoo.classifieds.com
> www.ezilonclassifiedads.com
> www.highlandclassifieds.com

Top things to know about Craigslist

- Craigslist is one of the most popular websites in the world, with around fifty billion page views per month.

- Most advertisements on Craigslist are free to post, but there are charges for certain categories in certain locations.

- Craigslist has rules for advertisers in order to keep it from becoming overloaded with spam. The most important rule is that you may only post to one category and in one city, no more than once every forty-eight hours.

- Craigslist has a policy against anyone posting for another person as an agent or posting service.

- Craigslist has a very good system for keeping contact information anonymous between possible buyers and sellers.

- Besides advertisements, Craigslist also has very popular forums.

- Craigslist is a local service. You choose the city or region in which you want to advertise.

Summary

Most important things to know from this section

- YouTube presents a great opportunity for businesses to gain free exposure.

YouTube, Email Marketing, Podcasting, & Craigslist

- Your YouTube videos can be great vehicles for driving traffic to your website.

- Email marketing is a highly effective way to keep your business on the minds of people.

- Email marketing does not mean renting a list of addresses and spamming them on a regular basis. It means creating your own list of people who have agreed to receive your emails.

- Sending marketing emails to people who have not agreed to receive them is called spamming. Spamming is illegal unless you follow the strict guidelines of the Can-Spam Act of 2003 (www.brickway.net/can-spam-act/).

- Spamming doesn't work because of modern email filters, and the general distaste of the public for unsolicited mail.

- One of the best ways to build an email list is to offer a discount or free gift for signing up.

- Podcasts may include audio and/or video, and are an immensely popular type of broadcasting.

- In some ways, podcasts are similar to blogs. They may include whatever type of content the owner wants, can be whatever length the owner wants, and be created at whatever time intervals the owner chooses. Also, podcasts work with RSS (really simple syndication).

- Podcasting is a great way to establish yourself as an expert.

- Podcasts can be a great vehicle for driving traffic to your website.

- Craigslist is one of the most popular websites in the world, with around fifty billion page views per month.

- Most advertisements on Craigslist are free to post, but there are charges for certain categories and in certain locations.

- Craigslist has rules for advertisers in order to keep it from becoming overloaded with spam. The most important rule is that you may only post to one category and in one city, and no more than once every forty-eight hours.

Most important things to do

- Open a free YouTube account and upload a couple of videos to get exposure for your business.

- Carefully choose tags for your videos that will cause them to be visible when someone searches for those keywords.

- Start an email marketing campaign ASAP. Set up your website to deliver a free gift of some sort to those who "opt-in" to receive it.

- Use an email marketing service to make your campaign easy to run.

- Consider whether podcasting is for you. It's a great way to promote your expertise and drive traffic to your website, but requires a continuous investment of time.

- Try using Craigslist to grow your business. Test a few different approaches to see if it can be a good marketing vehicle for you.

Most important things NOT to do

- Ignore the power of YouTube

- Ignore the effectiveness of email marketing (This is an inexpensive and easy way to keep your business on the minds of people.)

- Spam (Spamming is not effective, and is illegal unless you follow very strict guidelines.)

- Ignore Craigslist (There is a massive amount of traffic there. It's worth testing a few approaches to see what might work.)

Part 7–Ten Amazing Tools & Timesavers

One of my favorite quotes is from Mark Twain. In reference to the power of words, he said "The difference between the right word and the almost-right word is the difference between 'lightning' and 'lightning bug.'" I couldn't help but think of that quote for this section. The same principle also applies to tools. There is a huge difference in having the right tool and the almost-right tool. With the rapid pace of new technology and innovation, we need to make sure to use the best tools we can to help us work. They keep us more organized and save us time. The following ten tools and services are the best ones I know to help make your work (and life) easier.

> *Reality check*: Start gradually with these tools. Give them a test drive before deciding whether they are valuable enough for you to start using regularly and extensively.

Evernote

(www.evernote.com)

- One of the best pieces of software I've come across in recent years is Evernote. After using it for only a short time, I felt like I could never go back to not having it. It is extremely useful, easy to learn, easy to get, and free (unless you upgrade to a premium account).

- Evernote is a system for having practically all the information in your life at your fingertips. It is a database of the information you want to keep. It also synchronizes to all of your devices, so you have updated information wherever you are. Evernote has tons of great features that make it an amazing program, but these overall points summarize why it's so good:

    Inputting is a snap. It's practically effortless to put information into Evernote. You may input information in the form of a text note, an audio note, or a photo. Evernote even gives you a special email address so you can always forward an email into your database. If you see something you want to remember while surfing the web, you can take a screenshot in a flash. No need to give it a filename or decide where to save it. It automatically flows into your Evernote.

Accessing the information is easy. Tags are used for categorizing the notes, although they are not a necessity. Simply doing a search can usually pull up the note you are looking for. While performing the search, Evernote scans the text in the notes, and it can even read text that's in a photograph. For example, if you take a photo of someone's name and address on an envelope, it will flow directly into your Evernote database and be searchable by the text in that name and address.

Device synchronization. Your information is synchronized on all of your devices. You don't have to go looking from one device to another for the information you want. For me, this is a great convenience. Knowing that I need only look in Evernote on any of my devices saves me lots of time and hassle.

Notebook sharing. Evernote allows you to share notebooks with others. For example, my wife and I have a shared notebook. We can both put notes into it that the other might be interested in. We share shopping lists, appointment information, travel information, and even decorating ideas. If I see an item in a store that she might like, I snap a picture of it to go into our shared notebook. Then we can both see it and remember it whenever we want.

Gmail

(www.gmail.com)

Gmail is a free email service provided by Google. It first became available in 2007 and quickly became one of the most popular web email platforms. It has an amazing array of features that can keep you more organized, more productive, and less encumbered by clutter (like junk email). Besides its usefulness as an email platform, Gmail also works like a personal database. It allows you to easily search and find information from emails you've sent or received in the past. With its recent incorporation into Google Drive (Google's free cloud-based storage system), Gmail users are now given fifteen gigabytes of storage that may be shared with the other services offered under Google Drive.

Here are some of the great features of Gmail:

> **Search functions.** Organizing email used to mean creating folders for saving different messages. Gmail has such a robust system for searching emails that folders aren't necessary. You may search by various parts of an email: by subject line, message text, address, etc. You may search during particular time frames, and filter your results by including and excluding certain words.
>
> **Labels.** Labels are like tags you use to categorize your emails. You can set labels like "Facebook" for all notifications that come from Facebook, or "Amazon" for any email related to purchases you made on Amazon.com. Labels allow you to quickly see all of the emails from a certain person, place, type, or category. They also work well in conjunction with other features of Gmail, such as searches and filters
>
> **Filters.** Filters are simply fantastic. They allow you to automate certain things to save you time every day. With a filter, you can program actions to happen automatically whenever an email arrives. For example, if there are junk mail messages that you're tired of seeing, you can create a filter for them to be deleted automatically. If there are certain emails that you think an associate needs to see, create a filter to forward the messages automatically. You can also program some messages to skip the inbox. (For example, I have a label called "Amazon" and a filter set for messages from Amazon. com to skip my inbox. I don't need to read the messages every time I order something from Amazon.com. But if I want to read them, I can easily do so by clicking on that label name.)
>
> **Import email accounts.** Gmail allows you to import other email accounts, so they can be managed within your Gmail account. When you write emails you can decide which sender-address you want to show on the email. For example, I use Gmail to manage an AOL email account. When I reply to messages, I show the AOL

address as the sender. (This only works with email providers that allow POP3 access).

Elance

(www.elance.com)

Wouldn't it be great if you could find good, skilled workers to do work for you at a low price? Maybe you need a new logo designed. Perhaps you need some help writing articles for your blog. Or, it could be you want someone to create a custom app for your business. Enter the world of Elance. Elance is a website that connects skilled workers around the world with customers who need their services. It is an easy and safe system to use, with built-in protections for both the workers and their clients. Once you start using Elance, it's likely that you will never see the world of small business the same way again. It gives you simple, direct, immediate, and affordable access to people who can help you, for an hourly rate or a fixed price. Elance is used by approximately five hundred thousand businesses and has around two million freelance professionals available to be hired.

How does Elance work?

Here is a rough idea of how Elance works. Let's say you want to create an ecommerce website and you want someone to design it for you. First, you create a free account at www.elance.com. You are then able to post a job that workers around the world will be able to see and bid on. In your post, you will give a detailed description of the kind of website you want, and the type of freelancer you are looking for. Then you sit back and watch as bids for the work come in. You examine the bids and the bidders. You look at their ratings and reviews from past jobs, how many jobs they've done in the past through Elance, how much they've been paid so far through Elance, where they're located, and more. If you have a question to ask one of the freelancers before you hire him or her, you can send a message. The next step is to select one to hire. When you select one, you make an agreement with that person on various points, such as the price, start date, end date, and particular milestones for the project. When both parties consent, the agreed-to price must be paid by you to Elance. The payment will go into an escrow account and will only be released when you are satisfied with the work that was done. Once the funds have been put into escrow, the project moves into the work room. The work room is where communications are made about the project as it moves along. The work room features a message board for exchanging messages, file sharing, video conferencing, and HTTPS encrypted security. When the work has been completed to the customer's satisfaction, the customer releases the funds from the escrow account. Both the customer and the freelancer then give a rating and review of the other party, which will be a permanent part of their records on Elance.

Again, this is only a rough idea of how it works. There are variations to the ways I described above. For example, payment works differently for work done on an hourly rate versus a fixed price. Also, there are different ways of finding workers. You may simply browse to find workers based on their locations, specialties, prices, etc. and then invite only selected ones to bid on your job. There are various other features and options as well, including a paid option that will make your post more prominently visible to freelancers. This is meant to attract more bids for the project.

My experience with Elance

I personally have hired people on Elance about twenty times. Most of the time, I have been very happy with the results. The workers were truly skilled and professional. A couple of times I was not happy with the results and took measures to end the arrangement sooner than had been agreed. This may be done directly with the freelancer by renegotiating the terms of the project, or (as a last resort) by filing a dispute through Elance. Elance has a solid system for dealing with disputes. Since both parties have an interest in keeping their ratings on the positive side, disagreements are usually handled quickly and easily. Only one time have I filed a dispute with Elance (on some very poor-quality work). Once it was filed, the freelancer immediately backed-down and accepted that the funds would not be released.

It doesn't take long to get used to using Elance. You learn from experience. One thing I learned is that it is much better to audition freelancers before giving them big jobs. Try to create a small step for them to do first so you get an idea of their abilities, timeliness, communication skills, etc. Also, I've found that you often get what you pay for. You will see some extremely low bids for work sometimes. It is tempting to give those people a chance, hoping they will do a great job for very cheap. Some of them even have great reviews and ratings. My experience has been that (usually) the quality is not up to the level of my needs for those extremely low bids. Another thing I sometimes do is hire two people instead of one. I have done this several times for logos. This way, I can compare the work and go with the one I like better.

Here is a sample list of freelancing specialties you can find on Elance

- Web design
- Flash animation creation
- Voiceover work
- Proofreading
- Newsletter creation
- Translation
- Press release writing and submission
- Speech writing
- Architecture
- Contracts and legal documents
- Bookkeeping
- Print ad design
- Original music creation
- AdWords management
- iPhone app creation
- Market research
- Competitive analysis
- Computer programming
- Facebook page creation

One very popular specialty on Elance is that of a virtual assistant (or "VA"). These are workers from around the world who specialize in doing whatever work you want them to do at a given time. Many businesses have a VA that keeps regular hours over the period of weeks, months or years. For example, you can hire someone to work for a certain amount of time every week. Perhaps you want someone to help with various aspects of Internet marketing (such as writing articles for your blog, doing research on your competition, or building citations). You can hire a VA to be your employee for those things for five or ten hours per week. This is an excellent way to free up time for other things. It might take a few "auditions" to find the right person, but you will be glad when you do.

Hootsuite

(www.hootsuite.com)

One of the biggest challenges with Internet marketing these days is to keep up a presence on social websites. As I mentioned in Part 5 of this book, the social web requires engagement. It's not a set-and-forget task. Using Facebook, Twitter, LinkedIn, etc. requires a continuous investment of time over a period of years. Since time is our most precious resource, finding a simpler way to keep up our social web presence can make all the difference. Hootsuite provides this simpler way. Hootsuite is a social web management system that allows you to conduct your social engagement from a single interface, rather than having to jump around to the different sites individually. The name Hootsuite comes from the French expression tout de suite, which means "at once." Besides giving you a single interface to manage your social web presence, Hootsuite provides an array of other features that help streamline, organize and analyze your activity. For example, you can write one post in Hootsuite and push it out to several accounts at once, such as Twitter, Facebook, and LinkedIn. You can also receive customized reports that give you detailed information about your followers, mentions, and other statistics to keep you informed.

In the Hootsuite dashboard, your information is organized by profiles, tabs and streams. Profiles are things such as Facebook accounts, Facebook pages, Twitter accounts, Google+ pages and so on. Tabs work like the tabs in your web browser: they separate and organize your streams. Streams are vertical columns that show information, such as your news feeds. Streams are particularly useful because you can set a wide variety of things to be a stream, such as Facebook group feeds, Twitter mentions, or Twitter direct messages.

Hootsuite has a free version and a professional version. The free version has enough features to be very useful but is more limited. It limits you to five social network profiles, while the pro version allows you to have up to fifty. The pro version also offers more advanced message scheduling, meaning you may create your posts and then schedule them to be automatically posted at times you choose.

Other features of Hootsuite

- **Apps and Extensions.** Hootsuite has an extensive directory of apps and extensions that allow you to manage a large number of social web outlets. There are apps for managing YouTube accounts, Pinterest, Gmail, Trendspottr, Instagram, Tumblr and other services. There are also browser extensions that make sharing links you come across online faster and easier.

- **Team Support.** Hootsuite has great support for teams. There are several different permission levels that grant access for viewing or publishing on your behalf.

- **Mobile Apps.** Hootsuite has mobile apps for iPhones, Android phones, and iPads.

- **Hootsuite University.** This is Hootsuite's program for learning more about the social web and how to use Hootsuite to manage it.

- **Analytics and Listening Tools.** You can perform and save advanced searches, filter for certain content, and manage lists of followers. You can create search streams by keywords, mentions, hashtags, and more.

- **URL Shortener.** Since Twitter allows only 140 characters per tweet, a Hootsuite tool can be used to shorten the length of URLs. It's a system of substituting a shorter link for a longer one, while still directing to the same place.

- **Security.** No matter the type of device from which you access the Hootsuite dashboard, you have the protection of HTTPS to keep your passwords and profiles secure.

Jing

(www.techsmith.com/download/jing/)

Jing is a simple and free software program that serves a very handy purpose: it allows you to take screenshot photos of all or part of what's on your computer screen. It also allows you to record video of what's on your computer screen for a period of up to five minutes. You may then post these photos or videos directly to Facebook or Twitter, or easily send them as email through Jing.

Screenshot photos are very helpful. For example, suppose you just created a new Google AdWords ad, and want to remember the wording without having to go into AdWords every time. With Jing, you can quickly capture a photo of the ad and keep it where you can access it quickly. Or suppose you are looking at some flight details for your next trip but you only want to print the actual schedule, not all the junk information that goes along with it on the web page. Just use Jing to take a screenshot photo of the schedule and print the PNG photo.

In the case of video, Jing is great for remembering exactly how to do something or explaining it to someone else. For example, if your co-workers tend to get confused about uploading media into WordPress, you can have a Jing video show the steps it takes to do it. That way they don't need to bother you every time they get stuck.

> *Side-note fact:* Evernote also has a screenshot capture function but does not allow video recording.

How to use Jing to take screenshots or record video
1. When Jing is running, you see a small, yellow semi-circle at the top of your screen (it looks like a sun). When you mouse over it,

you will see three options: Capture, History, and More. Choose Capture (on the left) which has the crosshairs icon.

2. You will then be able to drag and select an area of your screen to capture.

3. After you have selected an area of your screen, you are given choices for what to do with that area. The choices are: capture image, capture video, re-do selection or cancel.

- If you select image, you will be able to name the file and save it to the location of your preference.

- If you select video, you will see a three-second countdown before recording begins. The recording can go as long as five minutes. When you are ready to stop recording, click the stop/finish button. You will then be able to name the file and save it to the location of your preference. (Jing video files are in the .swf format and should be able to play on your web browser—Microsoft Internet Explorer, Safari, Firefox or Google Chrome, etc..)

Other Features of Jing

- If you mouse over the sun and choose History, Jing can help you manage and reuse your captures. (Note, however, that if you delete a capture from your History, it will also delete the actual content from wherever you saved it on your computer.)

- To make Jing more effective for your needs, you can customize the buttons. For example, if there are three different folders where you save your screenshots you may create three different save buttons.

- You can annotate and markup your screenshots with text, arrows, framed areas, and highlighted areas. Once you select the area of your screen to be captured, select the image button. You are then given several tools (again on the left of the screen) to annotate and markup your image. (Videos cannot be annotated.)

- You can create a Facebook button for easy uploading to Facebook.

- You can create a Twitter button for easy uploading to Twitter.

IFTTT

(www.ifttt.com)

There are a lot of clever services on the Internet. Many are downright brilliant. IFTTT (pronounced "ift") has one of the most inspired concepts on the web, and can be a very handy tool for you. IFTTT stands for *"If This Then That."* IFTTT is a service for triggering automatic actions and information-flow between your most commonly used web and software services. The formulas for setting up these actions are called *"recipes."* The recipes are all based on the concept of *"If this happens, then that should happen."* The this part represents the trigger. The that part represents the action. Pieces of data in the trigger are called *ingredients*. The services connected by the recipes are called *"channels."* IFTTT offers over sixty channels you may use in your recipes: Twitter, Facebook, Evernote, Dropbox, Google Docs, text messaging, email, weather apps, and many more.

The purpose of IFTTT is to automate certain tasks, in order to save you the trouble of having to do it yourself regularly and manually. Recipes may be turned on or off.

Here are some examples of recipes you can set up in IFTTT:

- Create a searchable backup of every tweet you make automatically. In this recipe, Twitter connects with a Google spreadsheet.
- Send documents from Dropbox to your Kindle automatically whenever you place any PDF or DOC file in a certain folder.
- Automatically receive your iPhone camera photos to your email account.
- Backup your iPhone contacts to a Google spreadsheet automatically.
- Set your iPhone reminders app to automatically send reminders to Evernote. You can use Siri to set the reminder.
- Send people you meet a "nice to meet you" email automatically whenever you add them to your iPhone contacts

- When a certain person sends an email to your Gmail account, receive a text message automatically.

- If you receive an email from a specific address, blink the household lights to notify you. (This can be done if you use Philips Hue Connected bulbs).

- Add your Foursquare check-in history to your Google Calendar automatically.

- Automatically receive a text message of the day's weather forecast every morning.

- If the pollen count rises above a certain level, receive a notification so you can take a Benadryl. (The IFTTT weather channel keeps track of the pollen count.)

- Automatically add receipts that come through email to a Google spreadsheet or to Evernote.

- Set your email to automatically send all attachments to Dropbox or Evernote.

- If you change your Facebook profile picture, automatically change your Twitter profile picture too.

This is just a small sample of the recipes that can be set in IFTTT. There are thousands of pre-made recipes on the IFTTT website and you can create your own. You can even create a daisy chain of triggers and actions across several web services. There are almost limitless possibilities for automating tasks through IFTTT.

Dropbox

(www.dropbox.com)

While going to M.I.T., Drew Houston (the founder of Dropbox) had the bad habit of forgetting to bring his USB flash drive with him to class. This annoying problem caused him to think of a way that he could easily have his data with him wherever he went. He thought of a solution that would do just what he wanted. He felt it was a good enough solution to

Ten Amazing Tools & Timesavers

be turned into a business. The solution he thought of became the basis for creating Dropbox.

Dropbox is a software program you install on your computer. It gives you a folder called your "Dropbox." Whatever files you save in your Dropbox will be available on any of your other devices that have the Dropbox app installed. It's that simple. If you don't have any of your devices with you, you may use someone else's computer to log into your Dropbox account to access your files through the website. Dropbox is free to use for up to five gigabytes of storage. There is a cost to increase the storage amount.

The four most important functions of Dropbox are:

1. You can access data from any of your devices or from any computer over the web.
2. Putting your data in Dropbox creates a backup of your work in the cloud.
3. Dropbox makes it very easy to share your data.
4. You can access deleted and previous versions of your files.

When it comes to sharing your data, Dropbox makes it easy to share files or whole folders. You create a shared folder and add other people to it. The folder will then appear in the Dropbox of those people. You can share with non-Dropbox users also by getting a link to any file or folder. Once you get the link, you can send it to someone by email, Facebook, Twitter, instant message, or other ways. Facebook now offers integration with Dropbox. This allows you to share data from your Dropbox in Facebook's group pages without exiting the Facebook interface.

The ability to access deleted and previous versions of files is a very useful feature as well. Dropbox saves a history of all files and file versions for thirty days after deletion, or after changes have been made. By adding the "Packrat" feature in Dropbox, you get access to unlimited deletion and version history.

Remember The Milk

(www.rememberthemilk.com)

Remember The Milk is a web-based system for organizing your tasks and schedule. If you ever have trouble keeping track of your to-do list, Remember The Milk might be just the answer for you. It's free to use, although you can upgrade to a paid subscription for more freedoms and features. Two things that make Remember The Milk especially handy are: integration with other software programs, such as Microsoft Outlook, Google Calendar, Gmail, Google Maps, Evernote, Twitter, Siri and more, and the ability to synchronize your task lists to all of your devices.

After you log into your account, the first screen you'll see is the tasks screen. This is where you manage your tasks. To add new ones, click in the "Add Task" field and type in a name for your task. You can also add properties, such as the due date, priority, or any tags to make the task easy to find by searching. When a task is selected on the task screen, you may perform various other actions on it, such as marking it as complete or postponing it.

You can make custom lists of tasks. You may create as many lists as you want, for whatever purpose. When opening a new account, you're given five lists to start with: Inbox, Personal, Work, Study, and Sent. The Sent list stores the tasks you've sent to other people using Remember The Milk. One list will be marked as your default list, which will be the first list that shows up after you log in.

One of the most important features of Remember The Milk is that you can set reminders for your tasks. You have a variety of options for setting reminders. You can set them to notify you when a task is due, or within certain time intervals before a task is due. You can also choose from several methods to receive your reminders, including text message, email, or instant messenger (on services like AOL, MSN, Skype and Yahoo).

Adding new tasks can be as easy as sending an email. Your Remember The Milk account assigns you an email address. When you send an email to that address, the email automatically converts to a task in your inbox list. You can also use Siri on Apple's iOS devices to add tasks. Just tell Siri to add a task and it will appear in Remember The Milk.

Google Keyword Planner

(www.adwords.google.com)

In Part 3 of this book, I covered PPC (pay-per-click) advertising. In Part 4, I covered SEO (search engine optimization). I'll throw another cool acronym at you now: SEM. SEM stands for "search engine marketing." SEM is a broader category that encompasses both PPC and SEO. Doing SEM means marketing your business through the search engines in any shape or form. The most important and fundamental aspect of SEM is the keyword. After all, people use words when they perform searches. The point of SEM is to have your business become visible in the results when someone searches for what you offer. Whether it's SEO or PPC, choosing the right keywords can make all the difference. This process should be done slowly, carefully, and methodically. It's a bit like laying the foundation of a house—everything will be built on top of it. You don't want to realize later that you built it in the wrong place.

In the case of SEO, your keywords are more of a long-term investment. Good keyword research is the best groundwork for vital aspects of your website, including domain name, page titles, page headings, and content. PPC advertising, such as on AdWords, is much more flexible. You can (and often should) make changes to the keywords you are using. Whether it's for SEO or PPC, it's important to carefully research your keyword options.

One of the best tools on the web for keyword research is the Google Keyword Planner. This tool is invaluable in aiding your research. It has powerful features and gives a great deal of information, but its main uses are to provide ideas for keywords related to your business, and to give estimates of how much traffic you might expect from using those keywords. Google's Keyword Planner tool is free to use, but you must have an AdWords account. To access the Keyword Planner tool, sign in to your AdWords account. Then click the "Tools and Analysis" drop-down menu and select "Keyword Planner."

How to search for keywords and ad group ideas

1. Sign into your AdWords account, then click the Tools and Analysis drop-down menu and select "Keyword Planner."

2. Click Search for new keywords and ad group ideas to expand the search section.

3. Enter one or more of the following in the boxes that appear.

   - Words or phrases that describe what you're advertising.
   - The URL of a page on your website.
   - A category relevant to your product or service.

4. You will then see two tabs of information—keyword ideas and ad group ideas. Use the historical statistics to help you decide the value of those keyword and ad group ideas for you.

How to get search volume information for a list of keywords

If you have a list of keywords and want to know how often they are searched on Google, here's how:

- Sign into your AdWords account, then click the Tools and Analysis drop-down menu and select "Keyword Planner."

- Click Get search volume for a list of keywords or group them into ad groups

- Enter the keywords (one per line, or separated by commas) or upload a CSV file with your keywords.

- Click Get search volume to get historical statistics, which will bring up monthly search volume or competition data for your keywords. To see the keywords grouped into ad groups, click on the Ad group ideas tab in your results.

- Use filtering to show the information you are most interested in (see Targeting and filtering your results below).

Multiply keyword lists

Multiplying keywords can be an important aspect of keyword research. This is tedious to do manually, but can be done very quickly with a good tool. Multiplying keywords is about listing all possible combinations. For example, you might have a list of ten different colors and a list of four different t-shirt sizes. Using a keyword multiplier, you can create a list of all possible keyword combinations of colors and sizes. It will also give you historical statistics and traffic estimates for these new keywords.

Here's how to multiply keyword lists in Google's Keyword Planner:

1. Click Multiply keyword lists to get new keyword ideas.

2. In the List 1 box, enter your keywords, one per line or separated by commas.

3. In the List 2 box, enter a different list of keywords that you want to combine with List 1. (To multiply more than two lists, click the "X" to add more boxes.)

4. Click Get estimates to get traffic estimates, including estimated clicks or impressions for your combined keyword phrases. Or, click Get search volume to get historical statistics, such as monthly search volume or competition data for your combined keyword phrases.

Targeting and filtering your results

The Google Keyword Planner tool lets you refine your keyword ideas by targeting or filtering your results. You can target your results by location, language, and network settings. And you can filter your results by historical statistics, keyword options, or choose to include or exclude certain keywords.

To target your results, edit the settings on the targeting panel. You can edit the geographical locations, language settings, and network settings. Geographical locations can be countries, territories, regions, and cities. By clicking the nearby link you can get ideas for other locations that are nearby.

To filter your results, click the pencil icon next to the three options. You can filter by historical statistics, by keyword options, or by including or excluding ideas. Historical statistics refers to the average monthly searches, average monthly costs-per-click, or competition data. Filtering by keyword options refers to keywords that are already being used in your account, or that you've added to your plan. Include or exclude ideas allows you to eliminate results from your lists based on certain words that you want to include or exclude.

LastPass

(www.lastpass.com)

For those of us who use the web for many different tasks—shopping, banking, social websites, email accounts, etc.—logging in and out of websites gets very tedious. Not only do we lose time, but it's a hassle to keep track of account usernames, passwords, and other login information. LastPass is a service that can help ease and speed up your work. Not only does it help with logging in to websites, it also speeds up the process of filling out forms on the web.

LastPass stores your login information in a secure cloud system. This is called your "vault." When you use the web, LastPass runs as an extension in your browser. As you go about your normal activities, LastPass will notice any time you are logging into a website or filling out a form. It will then ask if you want to save that information to your vault. Saving it can automate the process of logging in the next time you go to that website, or automate the process of filling out a similar form. When all of the login information you use is loaded into your vault, the only login information you will need to remember is for your LastPass account (thus the name "LastPass").

It is very fast and easy to add sites to LastPass. You have a few options that tell LastPass how to respond when you visit each site. You may give the site a unique name that you choose, mark a site as a favorite, or choose to assign that site to a group that you create. (For example, you might have one group called "Banking" and another called "Shopping.") You may also choose whether to have LastPass log in automatically (auto-login) or be required to type the password each time yourself (Require Password Re-prompt). Requiring password re-prompt is a more cautious approach. It's best to use that option for accounts that require higher security, such as financial ones.

Features of LastPass

- LastPass can create high-quality passwords for you.

- In your vault, you can monitor information about the times your passwords have been used. You can also edit, share, and delete passwords.

- You can search by URL and username to find passwords in your vault.

- LastPass has an extension available for all of the following browsers: Internet Explorer, Firefox, Safari, and Google Chrome.

- LastPass has a premium service that allows you to use it on a mobile device.

- For filling out forms quickly, LastPass creates profiles that store your address, phone number, email, and other information. You can save several different profiles.

- You can import or export your saved login information.

- You can create and store one-time passwords (OTPs) for logging in on potentially insecure public computers.

- For more intense security, you can turn on multi-factor authentication that links your account to a fingerprint reader, USB key, or smart card reader.

Summary

Most important things to know from this section

- Evernote is an amazing tool for keeping your notes, lists and other information organized. It's super-easy to input information and to access it again. It synchronizes to all of your devices, and it's free to use (although there is a premium version).

- Gmail is a powerful email platform that can work like a personal database. Its search functions make it easy to find past messages and data. It allows you to manage email accounts from other providers, including writing and replying using those other addresses. Filters allow you to pre-program actions to be taken with emails from certain addresses, or that have certain words.

- Elance is a service for outsourcing jobs to skilled freelancers around the world. It is a very reliable and user-friendly system. It's free to open an account and post a job. Freelancers from around the world can bid on the job you post.

- Hootsuite provides a dashboard for managing many social web profiles at the same time. It can significantly reduce the amount of time and effort required to maintain your social web presence. It's free to use, but has a premium version.

- Jing is a simple and free software program for capturing screenshots from your computer screen. It can also capture videos from your screen of up to five minutes in length. It is very handy for saving or sharing information that shows on your computer screen at any time.

- IFTTT stands for "If This Then That." It is a web service that allows you to automate common actions you might take on your iPhone, Twitter, Evernote, Gmail and many other services. You create recipes that trigger automated actions between different software and services you use.

- Dropbox provides an easy way to keep your data current on all devices, and backed up in the cloud at the same time. A folder on your computer is called your "Dropbox." Whatever you save to that folder will be in the cloud, available on the web, and synchronized to all of your devices. It's free for a limited amount of storage space.

- Remember The Milk is a web-based system for organizing your tasks and schedule. It allows you to schedule reminders, and it offers integration with other services like Google Calendar, Gmail, Evernote, Siri, and more.

- The Google Keyword Planner tool is invaluable for doing keyword research. It can and should be used for research on SEO and PPC campaigns. To use it, you must have an AdWords account (which is free, and can be inactive).

- LastPass speeds up your tasks on the web by storing your login information for different websites. It can log you in automatically, and can also automate the process of filling out forms on the web. It's free to use, but has a premium version that allows you to use it on a mobile device.

Most important things to do

- Give these tools and services a test drive.
- Use Evernote. It takes a little time to find your own way with it, but it's well worth the trouble.
- If you are going to do any SEM (search-engine-marketing), you should use Google's Keyword Planner tool to do research. This process should be done slowly and carefully. All good SEM campaigns are built on proper keyword research.

Most important things NOT to do

- Over-do it. (Take a gradual approach toward testing these tools and services. If you find them helpful, work them into your routine gradually.)
- Rush the keyword planning process for SEO or PPC.
- Organize your information in a single-device fashion, without cloud connection. (Evernote, Dropbox, Remember The Milk, and even Gmail provide ways to keep your information accessible on a mobile device, or with any computer connected to the web.)

Part 8-Ten Timeless Marketing Principles

The world of marketing has changed dramatically in recent years. Technology has created more opportunities than ever to help businesses become more visible. But in the wide and turbulent ocean of changes, it is good to know that some things don't change. Marketing is still about capturing the interest of people and communicating a message. The following ten principles are established, proven and timeless. Many will seem familiar because they are used in many (or most) of the advertisements you've seen throughout your life. Be sure to apply these principles to your own marketing efforts to reach the next level of success.

Sell Benefits (Not Features)

This is one of the most important marketing principles in existence. It is simple, but commonly overlooked by most amateur marketers. When we advertise, we are attempting to communicate a message that will attract customers. What should that message be? We may have a wonderful product or service to offer. We may understand why and how it would be of use to someone. Other people, however, don't know as much about it as we do—and they don't want to spend time learning. Therefore, an advertiser needs to get the maximum impact from any attention their ads receive. While many advertisers push the features of a product or service, pushing the benefits is the way to get that maximum impact.

What's the difference between a feature and a benefit? A feature is a quality or technical aspect of something. A benefit is how that quality or technical aspect can benefit people. For example, a feature of a sports car might be that it has a five-hundred horsepower engine. The benefit is that it can go from zero to sixty MPH in under five seconds. Simply put, the benefit is what the product or service can do for the buyer. Advertising the benefit helps spark the imagination of prospective buyers, and hopefully gives them a feeling of "that would make some part of my life better!"

Here are a few more examples of features translated into benefits:

Ten Timeless Marketing Principles

Feature	Benefit
A vacuum cleaner has stronger suction	Spend less time vacuuming!
An MP3 player has 8GB of memory	It holds over 5,000 songs!
Tires have an advanced tread design	Safer and better handling in rainy conditions.
A mattress has individually wrapped coils	Better support so your back feels better.

If we are familiar with a product or service, we tend to think the benefits will be obvious. But remember, people aren't giving it much thought. They have other things on their minds. If you want their attention, you need to clearly communicate how your product or service will be a direct and significant solution for them.

Here are some benefits that could be attributed to products we see:

- It will make you feel more free (by saving you time).
- It will make you feel more loved (by connecting you with others).
- It will make you feel more respected (by learning a new skill to display).
- It will make you feel richer (by saving you money).
- It will bring excitement to your life (from action and adventure).
- It will make you feel more energy.

Spark their imagination

One of the best marketing tips I have ever come across was in an article about selling houses. The tip was: buy a brand-new propane grill. The idea was that when prospective buyers look around the house, the grill will spark their imaginations and lead to a positive feeling. Sparking imagination in order to lead to emotions is our primary goal in marketing. After all, the product is not what people are most concerned with. They are concerned with how buying the product will make them feel. And who doesn't feel good thinking about barbecuing for themselves and their family? (Needless to say, I took this advice. I had no trouble selling the house, and I believe that the grill did its job by sparking imagination.)

Selling the benefit appeals to emotions, and emotion is the gateway to making a buying decision. As the expert sales trainer Zig Ziglar says, "People usually buy on emotion and then they justify it with logic." Another way of expressing this principle is in the old maxim, "*Sell the sizzle, not the steak.*" What sparks your imagination more: a cut of meat, or a cut of meat sizzling on a grill? (My apologies to any vegetarians for this example.)

This doesn't mean the features shouldn't be mentioned. They can, and often should play a supporting role. As Zig Ziglar says, people justify their emotional decisions with logic. The important thing to keep in mind, however, is that it's the benefit and emotional appeal that are in the driver's seat for buying decisions.

Discover your USP

We are surrounded by all kinds of noise in today's world. We are bombarded with information on a daily and even hourly basis. As an advertiser, how do you break through the noise? It's not easy to do, but it's absolutely necessary to try. The first step in trying to stand out is to discover your USP, or "*unique selling proposition.*" Your USP is what makes your ads stand out from the others. It tells people the reason why they should do business with you, instead of your competitors. Discovering your USP can add new focus and purpose to the way you serve your customers, and how you advertise your business.

Here are some examples of USP's:

- Lowest price, guaranteed.
- Only service that offers a two-year warranty.
- Delivered in three days or less.
- Free iPod with purchase over $200.
- 24/7 customer support.

Discovering your USP is not always an easy process. There is also some risk involved. The purpose of a USP is to offer a benefit that separates you from your competitors. This inherently narrows your target market because the benefit you are promoting may not be of interest to some of your prospective customers. They might be looking for a completely different benefit, and be put off by your USP. Although your target market may be narrowed as a result, your USP should have a net-positive effect by finding more customers who are drawn to what you are offering.

Helpful ways to discover your USP

Discovering your USP is an important process that should not be rushed. You should consider a wide range of options and possibilities. You should consider short and long term aspects that a USP can bring. Once you discover the one that feels right, you will want to gear your whole marketing strategy to revolve around that USP. Although you could decide to change it sometime down the line, it is much better to stick with one consistently over time. Of course, there is no way to know for sure if the USP will be as effective as you hope. But doing some healthy research will be worth your while. If possible, find a way to test it on a small scale before going full force with it in all of your marketing efforts.

Here are some questions that can help you discover your USP:

- Is there a certain way that your product is different or superior?
- Does your business have a process that's unique?
- Is your pricing or pricing structure different and beneficial to the customers?
- Do you (or can you) offer a warranty or guarantee that would help you stand out?
- Is your customer service something that could give you a leg up on your competition?
- What's different about the way you deliver your products or services?
- Can you offer a free gift to every customer?

- What do your customers like about doing business with you?

Repetition

In essence, advertising is about communication. If our products or services are to be sought out by the public, our ads must be presented in a way that looks established, credible, and memorable. One of the most common mistakes businesses make is to advertise inconsistently and sporadically, rather than in a fluid and continuous way. Seeing an advertisement for the first time is like seeing a stranger: we don't know them, and they don't have credibility with us. On the other hand, seeing an advertisement on a regular basis creates familiarity, which helps build credibility. The business then seems less like a stranger, and more like an established part of the community.

Besides building credibility, repetition serves the purpose of reminding people over and over what you have to offer. They may see it and consider it several times before they decide to take action. Think about the ads you see often on television and in the newspaper. How often do they motivate you to make an immediate purchase? Only on rare occasions, right? Yet those ads continue to run, and run, and run. It's the cumulative effect of repetition that builds the credibility of those businesses in our minds, reminds us of what they have to offer (including their USP), and helps us think of them when we are interested in their type of product or service.

In 1885, British businessman Thomas Smith wrote a book called Successful Advertising. Here is an excerpt from the book that describes the way repetition works for ads:

The first time people look at any given ad, they don't even see it.
The second time, they don't notice it.
The third time, they are aware that it is there.
The fourth time, they have a fleeting sense that they've seen it somewhere before.
The fifth time, they actually read the ad.
The sixth time they thumb their nose at it.
The seventh time, they start to get a little irritated with it.
The eighth time, they start to think, "Here's that confounded ad again."

The ninth time, they start to wonder if they're missing out on something.
The tenth time, they ask their friends and neighbors if they've tried it.
The eleventh time, they wonder how the company is paying for all these ads.
The twelfth time, they start to think that it must be a good product.
The thirteenth time, they start to feel the product has value.
The fourteenth time, they start to remember wanting a product exactly like this for a long time.
The fifteenth time, they start to yearn for it because they can't afford to buy it.
The sixteenth time, they accept the fact that they will buy it sometime in the future.
The seventeenth time, they make a note to buy the product.
The eighteenth time, they curse their poverty for not allowing them to buy this terrific product.
The nineteenth time, they count their money very carefully.
The twentieth time prospects see the ad, they buy what is offered.

Here is another great quote from the 1800s. This one is from P.T. Barnum, the legendary showman and one of the greatest marketers in America history.

> *Advertising doesn't pay when it is done sparingly and grudgingly. Homeopathic doses of advertising will not pay – perhaps it is like half a portion of physic, making the patient sick, but affecting nothing. Administer liberally, and the cure will be sure and permanent. Some say "they cannot afford to advertise"… they mistake – they cannot afford not to advertise.*

Since most people have busy lives, it's not easy to communicate information to them that will be easily remembered. That's why repetition in your marketing efforts is essential for making progress. Ultimately, your goal should be for people to think of your business whenever they think of the type of products or services you offer.

Use Images

The importance of using good images in your ads can't be overstated. The old saying *"a picture is worth a thousand words"* certainly applies to advertisements. So much can be communicated and conveyed through images. It's no wonder television and magazines are such effective advertising mediums. Next time you watch television or read a magazine, pay close attention to the way the images are used. Ask yourself: *What message are they trying to communicate? What emotions are they trying to convey? How do they make me feel?*

People have been using images to communicate for thousands of years. Consider the hieroglyphics of Ancient Egypt. Their form of written communication relied heavily on images that represented recognizable aspects of their lives.

Here are some of the many benefits to using images in your ads:

- Our eyes are naturally drawn to them.
- They can show emotion on people's faces.
- The can convey a wide range of feelings with their use of colors, shapes, objects, etc.
- They allow people to clearly see what something is, such as a product.
- They can pique curiosity.
- They can tell a story.
- They are often easier to remember than words.
- They can be used to show charts, diagrams and tables.
- They can be used to show comparisons, such as before and after pictures.
- They transcend language barriers.

One way that images can be particularly useful is on the social web. It's a fact that posted images get much higher response rates than text posts. They also get shared more often. After all, this makes sense. Sometimes it's easier to look at the pictures rather than read the (sometimes lengthy) posts from your friends. If you plan to incorporate social web services (like Twitter, Facebook, Google+ and LinkedIn) into your marketing, be sure to make images a regular part of your posting routine. Pinterest is another popular social website that is an image-only platform. Many businesses are taking full advantage of Pinterest by posting images that represent their products and services.

Where to find images

There is no shortage of images available to use in your advertising materials. However, there are legal implications regarding the images you use. It's important that you have the legal right to use the images. Here are some of your options:

Use your own photos. Taking your own photos might be a good option for you. It is not expensive to take photos and you won't have to consider the legal implications that are involved if the photo was taken by someone else.

Use stock-image services. Through stock-image services, you can find an incredible selection of images which can be used for a price. This can get expensive, but it's a quick and easy way to obtain the images you need. (For a list of some great stock-image services, go to www.brickway.net/photo-downloading-sites/).

Look for creative commons images. There are many people who take pictures and allow them to be used by others without requiring payment. A creative commons license service can fill you in on the details for those types of arrangements. Flickr is a site you can go to for finding creative commons photos. For more information, go to http://www.flickr.com/creativecommons/.

Hire a photographer. Images serve an important purpose, and the quality of the images certainly matters. Sometimes the best thing to do is hire a professional photographer to take the photos for you.

Humanize

When people quickly glance at marketing items (such as websites, Facebook pages, or print ads), what gets their attention? Images—especially images of human faces. We are always curious about people. We want to see what they look like, what they are wearing, how they live, what they do, etc. Wanting to connect with other humans is a strong and intrinsic characteristic of our species. Friendly interactions and relations with other people make us feel good. Seeing happy faces is generally appealing. Adding photos that show people's faces, or adding other humanizing elements (such as humor) can go a long way toward making your business look more appealing.

The opposite is also true. Ads that are devoid of human faces, humor, or emotion can be cold and unappealing. There is a popular saying: "People buy from people." Whatever the product or service involved, our curiosity tends to be about people. We might wonder:

- Who is it for?
- Who is buying it?
- Who is selling it?
- Who makes it?
- Who does it?
- Why do they do it?
- Who do they work with?
- How long have they been doing it?
- What made them want to do it?

Many websites include an "About" page to answer questions about the people running the business. An "About" page can be effective for humanizing your website. Studies have shown that "About" pages are often looked at by visitors before making buying decisions. Besides having a good "About" page, be sure to humanize your other web pages and marketing materials as well.

Ideas for humanizing your marketing items

- Include photos that show happy faces.
- Write text that comes across as conversational, as opposed to dry and technical.

- Let your friends and fans get to know the people you work with.
- Do you have a hobby like playing golf or watching football? Insert something about it on your website.
- Have a contest among your employees and let your customers see pictures and results.
- Use social websites to post photos of things happening with the people involved in your business.
- Tell stories (more about that in the next section Tell Stories).
- Add a little humor.

Tell Stories

"*Facts tell, stories sell*" is one of the great marketing maxims. Storytelling is undoubtedly one of the most powerful elements you can use in your marketing efforts. People love stories. We watch television shows, read books, watch movies, and read newspapers for stories. We watch the nightly news to hear "today's top stories." Stories tap into our innate curiosity about events. When we hear about an event, we can't help but think: *What happened next?*

Successful marketers have been using stories to sell products for thousands of years. Why do stories help in marketing? For one thing, stories get people's attention. They hear about a person who is in a particular situation (having a problem, perhaps) and are curious to know more. This is how movies keep audiences in suspense for so long. People are anxious to know what will happen, and how situations will be resolved. Stories also have the power to communicate messages. They can be informative and instructive, and they are much more easily remembered than typical ad copy.

How to use stories in your marketing

To use a story for marketing, the only limit is your creativity. Here are some ideas for stories you could tell in your marketing efforts:

- A story about how you started your business

- A story about why you started your business
- A story about a lesson you learned
- A story about how your product or service really helped someone (This could be in the form of a customer testimonial.)
- A story about how a product or service was developed
- A story about a problem you encountered, and your quest for a solution
- An inspirational story about overcoming difficult odds
- A story that creates a good versus bad scenario (If your business is selling mattresses, perhaps the bad guy could be represented by *neck and back pain*.)

Always Be Testing

To get the maximum bang for your buck in marketing, testing should always be part of the equation. When people see websites and advertisements, they have gut reactions to things like: color, images, layout, fonts, headings, and other aspects of the design. A subtle change in your web pages and other ads often makes a big difference in customer conversion. Making testing a regular part of your efforts is an investment that will definitely pay off. With testing, you will gradually learn what gets a better response from prospective customers—and you can bet that the results will often surprise you. I've heard that at any given time, Amazon.com has over two hundred tests running on its website. No wonder they are the world's largest online retailer. They never stop testing and finding ways to improve.

Testing might seem like a difficult and complicated process, but it doesn't have to be. All it takes is some thought and planning. The execution can be very simple. Start by thinking of one thing to test. Consider the marketing campaigns you are currently running or planning to run. What is one aspect of them that can be tested? For example, if you are sending a direct mailer on Mondays, perhaps you should test that against sending mailers on Fridays? Or, perhaps you can create two different versions of the mailer to see which gets the best response. Of course, you have to have some system for tracking results. This can be achieved in a number of ways. In the case of a mailer, you could have one version that has a certain discount offer and another version with a different one. Or, you could give each version a different phone number.*

One of the best ways to test your marketing offers and messages is with Google AdWords. AdWords allows you to A/B test many different aspects of your campaigns. You could have two different versions of your ad that rotate, to see which gets a higher CTR (click-through-rate) or conversion-rate. You could have just one version of an ad but two different versions of a landing page to learn which converts better. Landing page testing is one of the most important kinds of testing. The look and feel of your web pages can have great significance. The results you get from testing through AdWords can be applied to other aspects of your marketing, so that you can have better promotional offers, better landing pages and more effective keywords.

(* Warning: Avoid using a different phone number for your business on the Internet. Search engine rankings can depend on having a consistent NAP – or Name, Address, and Phone number – appearing for your business. See Part 4 "Citations" for more about the NAP.)

Types of testing

The best way to get started with testing is with simple A/B tests. A/B testing means comparing the results of two versions of something. One version is called version "A," and the other is called version "B." The older version is usually the "A" (called the control) and the "B" is the new version. You need to decide what metrics will be analyzed for the results—e.g., is it phone calls, website traffic, web purchases, etc.? A valuable type of testing is with email opt-ins. Try different versions of an email opt-in form on your website to see which gets a higher rate of response. Your decision of what to test will depend on your goals.

Another type of testing is called "multivariate testing." Multivariate testing allows you to test various aspects of a webpage or ad at the same time. So, instead of changing just one aspect (such as the wording of your email opt-in form) you can test several aspects simultaneously. This, of course, is a much more advanced type of testing and requires a higher degree of knowledge. It also requires a much higher rate of response in order to draw helpful data.

Ideas for testing your website

Testing should be a never-ending process. There are unlimited possibilities for testing, and sometimes small details can make a significant change in results. Here are some things you might want to try A/B testing on your website:

- Home page images
- Home page banner
- Logos
- Email opt-in form
- Headings
- Embedding a video
- Background color

Tools for testing

Google Analytics is a great service that can help you test various factors on your website. (See Part 2 for more information on Google Analytics.) There are other services available that can give you fascinating information about visitor activity on your website—information not available through Google Analytics. Many are very inexpensive and helpful. For a description of some website testing services, go to www.brickway.net/tools-for-testing/.

Scarcity

The principle of scarcity in marketing describes the tendency of people to be more motivated to make a purchase if they feel there is a limited supply, or a limited amount of time to act. Does this work? How often have you heard phrases like "Limited time only!" or "While supplies last!" or "You must call now!" in advertisements? My guess is that it works. Sometimes people have a desire to make a purchase, but are in no hurry to do so. But upon hearing that the availability might be limited, that is often a catalyst for their snapping into action. Scarcity can appeal to our emotions and be a strong motivator. Have you ever known a friend or family member who got a great deal on a purchase, causing you to think "I wonder if they have any more?" or "I wonder if I could get the same deal if I act quickly?" People have a natural desire to get in on things that are limited or exclusive. We also like to feel that we are "keeping up" and not falling behind on the latest deals.

As a business, using the principle of scarcity can be beneficial in your marketing. Is it manipulative? Of course it is. (Although sometimes supply truly is low and items are scarce; in that case, it's not manipulative, just opportunistic.) To manufacture and create a scarcity for your products or services is an age-old tactic that will never go out of style. Almost everyone knows and understands this; it's a part of the free-market culture. Consumers know this trick and can see it from a mile away. Although we know the trick of using scarcity tactics, we still let them lure us in. As long as we feel like we got a good deal, we're pleased with ourselves.

Businesses need to be cautious about using scarcity tactics. Customers like to feel that they got a good deal and not that they got suckered. Running a promotion based on scarcity should at least appear authentic. You don't want to run the same "limited time only" sale indefinitely. Think of the negative backlash it could have. People who made purchases may be left with a resentful feeling that they were tricked. The scarcity principle can also cause you to lose customers. For example, let's say a person is interested in buying a certain product. Then a business has a "one-day-only" sale for that product. If the person is unable to go shopping on the day of the sale, he or she might put it off indefinitely. Why pay full price when there was a sale price before? Nobody wants to feel like they missed out on something better.

Here are some ways you might consider using the scarcity principle in your marketing:

- Running limited time only sales or promotions
- Offering coupons that have an expiration date
- Creating proposals that have an expiration date

- Selling items by auction
- Making products available during specific windows of time only—like the Walt Disney Studios limited time releases of their classic movies
- Offering a seminar or workshop with an advertised (and limited) number of spaces available
- Creating an event that is invitation-only
- Advertising how many of a certain product you have in stock—e.g., "We have 6 in stock. When they're gone, they're gone!"

Listen First

Years ago, I was on an elevator with a man who was holding a painting in a nice frame. (The painting was in the nice frame, not him.) I made a remark about the painting, which started an interesting conversation. It turned out that he was an art-auctioneer. This was on a cruise ship, and his job was to sell artwork to the passengers. He was very friendly and frank. He admitted to me that the reason he was on the elevator holding the painting was that he found it was a good way to strike up conversations with people and invite them to attend his art auction. He said that he had been a salesman of one type or another for thirty years. I had always been interested in sales and marketing, so I took the opportunity to ask him this question: *What is the most common mistake people make in sales?* He answered that the most common mistake is assuming that they know what the prospective buyer cares about. For example, perhaps the salesperson starts rattling off information about the price, certain features, or certain benefits. This is called doing a *product dump*. Often times, it's none of these things that the prospective buyer cares about. People have all kinds of reasons for buying things; many of which are completely unpredictable. It's important to keep in mind that they might not be using it themselves, or they might not be paying for it themselves. Perhaps they want to buy it for a movie scene in which it will be crushed, set on fire, and thrown off a cliff. Every customer is different, and it's important to remember that they can have a wide variety of reasons for being interested. Rather than assume it's something obvious that they care about, it's much better to simply ask them and let them tell you.

I had another interesting experience recently at the dentist's office. It was my first time at this particular office and, naturally, I had to fill out several forms. One of the forms had questions like these: *What qualities do you like in a dentist? What are your biggest concerns when visiting a dentist? What do you want most from a dentist?* I'm not crazy about filling out forms, especially with questions like those. When the hygienist entered the room, I asked why those questions were on the form. She said it's so the dentist can customize the approach for each customer. It turns out that different people have very different feelings about dentists. Some people are afraid of dental work because they have had a painful experience in the past. Some are self-conscious about the appearance of their teeth. Some are worried about high costs. From a marketing perspective, I thought it was very clever to ask questions to find out what each customer cared about. Knowing what customers and prospective customers care about helps us serve them better. Whenever possible, find ways to listen to your customer before assuming that you know what they are most interested in and why.

Here are a few ways to be a better listener for the sake of marketing and serving your customers:

- Find a few questions that get people talking about what they want, and why they want it.

- Avoid yes or no questions. Open-ended questions are better, such as: *What brings you here today? What are your main concerns? How can we help you find what you are looking for?*

- While listening, don't try to craft an answer. Try to understand exactly what they are saying.

- Don't assume you know the rest of what they are going to say.

- Don't interrupt them.

- Pay attention to non-verbal cues.

- Try to be someone they can talk to, instead of someone who is constantly pushing an agenda.

Reciprocity

In psychology, the principle of reciprocity refers to the human tendency to want to give something back when something is received. If someone does a favor for you, it's normal to feel a sense of gratitude and want to reciprocate. The more we feel like their motivation was from kindness, the more we feel a desire to reciprocate. If we feel there are ulterior motives behind the favor, we are less inclined to reciprocate.

Using the principle of reciprocity for marketing purposes is very common in today's society. There are "free gifts" floating all around us. Businesses hope you will enjoy and appreciate their free gift and then reciprocate by becoming a customer. It's hard to go anywhere without being offered a free gift, even to your own mailbox.

Although it can be effective for marketing, the principle of reciprocity is not an easy one to leverage. As I mentioned above, we are constantly bombarded with offers. How often does this lead us to try, and then buy? Not that often, really. What does it take to make the principle of reciprocity work for your business? A great gift and a great product. Mediocre doesn't get you much in this area. The quality level needs to be very high on both counts. If the quality level is not high enough, you run the risk of leaving a negative impression.

What should you hope for as the result of using the principle of reciprocity in your marketing? A new customer would be great, but it can also be beneficial to add someone to your email marketing campaign. This way you will have permission to email them about your products or services (see more about email marketing in Part 6 of this book).

Is it overly-manipulative to market in this way?

The principle of reciprocity reflects the good nature in people. Wanting to return a kindness with a kindness is a way that people treat each other well. It's the Golden Rule—*Do unto others as you would have them do unto you.* It might seem wrong to try to exploit this part of a person's psyche for marketing. My suggestion is that you take a selfless attitude and try to give without expecting anything in return. Hopefully you feel a sense of purpose in your business from making things, fixing things, selling things, or performing services that people need. Apply that sense of purpose to some action or involvement that helps someone without expecting to profit from it. It's that kind of generous attitude that will be appreciated by others, and could be beneficial for your business. Ben Franklin said, "Being good to others is being best to yourself." That's great advice from one of America's first master-marketers.

Ways to apply the principle of reciprocity to your marketing

Here are a few ways you can use the principle of reciprocity for your business:

- Offer something for free, such as a product, service, or access to helpful information.
- Offer coupons.
- Give discounts.
- Try to greatly exceed customers' expectations for what you are offering.
- Be willing to teach something.

Summary

Most important things to know from this section:

- One of the most important principles in marketing is to communicate clearly and specifically how a product or service can improve part of someone's life. In other words, sell the benefits, not the features. For example, a feature of a vacuum cleaner might be that it has a powerful motor. The benefit might be that rugs get cleaner, and vacuuming gets done faster.
- Your USP, or unique selling proposition, tells people why they should buy from you instead your competitors. If you want them to give you their business, you need to give them the reason why they should. A good USP should be the centerpiece of all your marketing efforts.
- If your ad is only seen once by someone, it's not likely to be effective. Repetition is required to have a significant impact. The more they

are reminded of your business, the more likely they are to become your customers. Repetition also gives an appearance of stability and credibility for your business.

- Using images in your ads is very important. They can communicate messages, convey emotions, and let people clearly see what you're offering. They are very useful for social website posts. They get more attention, and are shared more often than other types of posts.

- People are more comfortable if they feel they are dealing with people and not just computer screens. Humanizing your website and advertising materials is very important. Adding images of people's faces, a bit of humor, and stories can go a long way toward making your ads more appealing.

- Stories are one of the most effective marketing tools. The old maxim "Facts tell, stories sell" is a great one to remember and apply. Stories pique curiosity and hold people's attention longer than typical ad copy. They can also have a clear message about the benefits of your products or services.

- Testing is a necessary part of any great marketing strategy. Good marketing becomes great by gradually learning what works better and what doesn't. You will often be surprised by the results. Changing large or small features can sometimes cause remarkable differences in response.

- The principle of scarcity in marketing describes the tendency of people to be more motivated to make a purchase if they feel there is a limited supply, or a limited amount of time to act. Using the scarcity principle is a very common tactic, and a normal part of the marketing culture. If it's used well, customers feel good about the deal they got. If it's not used well, they might feel resentful about being manipulated or "suckered."

- One of the biggest mistakes made in sales and marketing is to assume that you know what prospective customers care about. It's always best to ask questions and listen before pushing and promoting certain benefits. Whenever possible, listen first.

- The principle of reciprocity refers to the tendency to give back when something is received. It is not easy to leverage because we are constantly bombarded with "free" offers and gifts. It can be effective, but is largely dependent on the quality level of the gift, and whether the perceived impression is of generosity or manipulation. This principle is often used effectively to build lists for email marketing (e.g., give a free gift in exchange for a sign-up to your newsletter).

Most important things to do:

- Be sure to primarily promote benefits, as opposed to features.
- Discover your USP and use it to full advantage.
- Use images to draw attention, and convey messages and emotions.
- Humanize your marketing efforts with humor, images of people, stories, etc.
- Use stories to draw people's attention and promote the virtues of your products or services.
- Use scarcity tactics in a way that makes customers feel good about the deal they get.
- Always be testing. Marketing is a slow and gradual learning process. Testing is the key to greatness.
- Ask open-ended questions and listen intently before pushing or promoting certain benefits. Find out what buyers care about.

Most important things NOT to do:

- Advertise without promoting benefits.
- Advertise without a clear USP.
- Advertise without continuous repetition.
- Advertise without using images.
- Advertise without adding a human touch.
- Advertise without using stories.
- Advertise without running A/B tests.
- Assume you know what a prospective customer cares about.

Part 9-Ten Things Every Entrepreneur Should Know

How do you become a successful entrepreneur? You find a market and serve it well. This answer makes it sound so easy, but of course it isn't. Some lucky folks do stumble upon entrepreneurial success without much effort. There are a lot of stories about how people have fallen into something that worked more or less by accident. For example, I met a man who wanted to visit China at a time when visas were difficult to obtain. He decided to create an importing business for the sole purpose of getting a visa to visit China. His plan worked for getting the visa. What he didn't count on was finding immediate success with the importing business. By the time I met him, he had been a successful importer of electronics for over twenty years.

For most successful entrepreneurs, however, the road to success was no cakewalk. It took a great deal of struggle and stamina to make things work. There are many inspiring stories of people who went from struggle to success. We can learn a lot from those who have survived and thrived as entrepreneurs. In this section, I want to outline ten of the most important principles to understand and adopt on your road to success. They are:

The importance of time management
The importance of networking
The importance of planning
The importance of reputation
The importance of partnerships
The power of optimism
The power of persistence
The power of focus
The power of habit

The Importance of Time Management

Time is our most precious resource. To quote Ben Franklin, "Don't waste time, for that is the stuff that life is made of." Very true, Ben. But if only it were easy. Let's face it, managing our time is one of the biggest challenges in modern society. Our attention is pulled in so many different directions. We have become consummate multitaskers. Yes, it makes us feel very productive—but are we really?

While in New York City a couple of years ago, I learned an amazing fact: the Empire State Building was completed in 411 days. This happened during the years 1930-1931. I find that completely remarkable. Imagine the brilliant planning and execution involved in that accomplishment. Now that's what I call time management!

Accomplishing difficult goals takes work, and work takes time. There's no way around it. Because there's no way to add hours to the day, we need to find ways to manage the hours we have. Fortunately, there are ways to get control of our time.

The most important aspect of time management is prioritizing. It's been said that a lack of time is a lack of priorities. Having several goals that divide your time equally is a great way to become overwhelmed, overstressed, and unproductive. When you prioritize, it helps to make your goals as specific as possible. For example, instead of making the vague goal to "start blogging," make a goal to set up the blog and create five posts. When you are clearer in what you ask of yourself, your energy can be put to use in a more efficient way. You will not lose time to indecision about what you should be doing.

Prioritizing your goals is the most important aspect of time management. Even with clear priorities, however, it is easy to get distracted and sidetracked. Here are a few common workday time-wasters you should try to avoid in order to be more productive:

- Telephone interruptions
- Too frequent checking of email
- Too frequent checking of social websites
- Drop in visitors
- Unnecessary reading (that includes news and blurbs you see on web pages)
- Micromanaging

- Lack of organization

If you want to get control of your time, set clear priorities. Then make sure you devote most of your time to the top priorities. Sometimes this requires forceful elimination. You have to give up certain goals and activities. As soon as possible, do a thorough audit of how you spend the minutes and hours of your days. How much of that time is spent actually working on your top priorities? Spreading your energy on too many things will make it difficult to make progress on your top priorities.

"Time is really the only capital that any human being has, and the only thing he can't afford to lose." (Thomas Edison)

The Importance of Reputation

Reputation is one of the most significant assets of a business. It always has been and always will be. Some people think that if they work hard, they don't need to concern themselves with appearances. Unfortunately, though, it's not what you do that builds your reputation—it's what people see and perceive you to do. One of my favorite stories regarding reputation is of a young Ben Franklin living in Philadelphia. He had opened his own print shop and wanted to make a name for himself. To help do that, he deliberately rolled a cart of heavy paper rolls up Market Street on a regular basis so that people would see and perceive him as hard-working. He understood that it was not only important to be hard-working, but also to be seen as hard working.

Your reputation is an important asset, and should be protected as such. People are cautious about spending their money. They don't like to put blind faith in businesses they haven't heard any good things about. Businesses with good reputations can draw customers like a magnet because good reputations inspires trust and credibility.

The most important thing to understand about reputation is that it takes a long time to build a good one, but almost no time for it to be destroyed. Warren Buffet, the billionaire investor, understands this well. For the businesses he owns, he lets his managers know that if they lose money, he will be forgiving, but if they lose an ounce of reputation, he will be ruthless.

Social proof

To succeed in marketing, it helps to understand the factors people consider when making decisions. Our decision-making processes are very subjective. No two people have exactly the same way of thinking. However, studies have shown that certain psychological influences commonly affect our decision-making processes. One of the most influential psychological phenomena to affect our decision-making is called "social proof." Social proof, which is also referred to as "informational social influence," is known to affect the decision-making and behavior of people in various situations. It prompts our natural follow-the-leader tendency, and influences us to assume that the people around us possess a more knowledgeable understanding of a situation than we do. Social proof is what drives conformity. When we are not sure of ourselves, we observe others to help us choose an appropriate course of action.

A good example of using social proof in marketing is when McDonalds puts "*Billions and Billions Served*" on their signs. Signs of popularity, interaction, and engagement serve as social proof.

Here are a few examples of how you can use social proof in your marketing:

- Testimonials in your advertising materials
- Articles or content created by customers
- Social web business pages that show activity and engagement
- Reviews for your business (such as on Yelp) serve as social proof
- A feed from your Facebook page on your website
- Any indication that people are visiting your pages online, buying your products or services, and interacting in a positive way with your business

Your reputation online

Few things are as important in business as your reputation; and your online reputation is of critical importance. It's becoming more and more common for prospective customers to research businesses before making deals. Review sites like Yelp are gaining in popularity. Social websites can also have a colossal effect on your online reputation. Having a system for managing the reputation of your business is highly advisable. This means trying to cultivate positive reviews and mentions, as well as monitoring and dealing with negative ones. If a negative review shows up about your business, you can often mitigate the damage by crafting a response that will be visible to those who see the review. It could tell your side of the story, or it could be an acknowledgement of a mistake. Either way, it can demonstrate that you are engaged, thorough, and professional in how you conduct business.

Tools for managing your reputation online

If you want to monitor your reputation online (as you should), there are some very handy tools available. Some can be set to inform you when your company name or certain keywords appear on sites around the web.

> www.getfivestars.com
> www.google.com/alerts/
> www.alerts.yahoo.com
> www.twitter.com/search-home/
> www.socialmention.com
> www.trackur.com

The Importance of Referrals

Anyone who has been in business for a while knows how powerful word-of-mouth advertising can be. If you have existing customers who are happy with your products or services, getting referrals from those people can make your business thrive. Referrals and reputation are related but not the same. Having a good reputation can lead to referrals, but having a strategy for referrals is different than protecting your reputation. Referrals are something for which you should ask. A good reputation is not something for which you can ask (although you can ask for positive reviews, testimonials, etc.).

Referrals are of great value to your business, and happy customers are often willing to give them. The only thing standing in the way, sometimes, is the willingness of the business to ask for them. Learning to ask might take practice at first. You'll need to experiment with different ways, times, or situations to see which work best. Find a way that makes sense for you, and then apply it systematically. After a while, habit will kick in and you won't even think about it.

Some important questions to consider are: *How do I want customers to refer me? To whom do I want them to refer me? Are there certain words I want them to use?* Considering these questions is helpful and should lead to more referrals. You want to make it as easy as possible for everyone involved. Having some words written to give out (like a cheat sheet) can be a good idea. The more specific you are when you ask for a referral, the more likely the referrals will start flowing in.

Tips and ideas for getting referrals

- Have a systematic way of reminding customers that you appreciate referrals, and that they are the lifeblood of your business.
- Leave a few extra business cards with customers.
- Ask for referrals when you are face-to-face, if possible.
- Put "referrals appreciated" on your business cards and on your email signature.
- Set a goal, such as to increase your rate of referrals by 15%.
- Go the extra mile for your most appreciative customers by giving them extra service before asking for referrals.
- Express your thanks and appreciation to anyone that gives you a referral.

The Importance of Partnerships

It's been said that great successes are the result of great partnerships. I am a firm believer in that statement. No matter how brilliant, diligent, or capable a person may be, they cannot compete with a healthy team that works together. A good team can function on a much higher level than any individual. Working in harmony with others is a great experience because it brings out the best in everyone. Partners can motivate each other, support each other, and back each other up. Good partners can bring a variety of skill sets, past experiences, educational backgrounds, and ideas to a business. Consider the various parts of an automobile. Alone, each one can't do much, but if you put them together, you get a tremendous amount of power.

Of course, it's not an easy thing to create partnerships. In fact, it's one of the most difficult things to achieve. Working closely with others and tying your fortunes together can be stressful. It takes patience and fortitude for the partnership to survive through hard times. Deciding to be partners with someone is a big decision. You want to be open to it, but not rush into it.

Questions to ask before entering into a partnership:

- Do you agree on the same goals for the business?
- Are both partners equally motivated for the same goals?
- What are the benefits to each partner in joining together?
- Are there any communication problems or difficulties?
- Is there a way to keep all aspects of the business transparent, rather than rely on blind-trust?
- What's the end game?
- How will disagreements be resolved?
- Does anyone have the final decision?
- Can one partner fire the other?
- What happens if someone offers to buy the business?
- What are the metrics that will be used for measuring progress?
- Will either partner be investing their own cash?
- Will there be a detailed agreement in writing?

Antes que lo cases, mira lo que haces. (Spanish proverb meaning "Before you marry, you'd better watch what you're doing.")

Ten Things Every Entrepreneur Should Know

The Importance of Planning

One of the best things to learn as an entrepreneur is how to be a good planner. It's easy to get excited about business ideas and opportunities. Sometimes we want to start working to realize our dreams before taking the time to carefully measure, calculate, and plan what our actions will lead to (or won't lead to). Lack of planning is one of the biggest business mistakes you can make. Though many of us have already learned this lesson (the hard way), it's an easy one to forget. If we don't remember to look for this hidden trap, we usually fall into it. Rushing the planning process is like running through woods full of poison ivy: if we are not wary of the danger, we will probably suffer later.

Here are a few ways to help you succeed in making good plans:

Plan in stages

For several reasons, big goals should always be planned (and pursued) in stages. Another way of describing this is to say that your eventual goal will have a series of sub-goals; your sub-goals will have sub-sub-goals; all the way down to setting daily goals. Keep the stages and milestones toward your goal as simple and close together as possible. The closer together your milestones are, the more clearly you will see your path and your progress. The further apart, the more formidable and elusive progress will seem.

> *Life by the yard is apt to be hard. Life by the inch is more of a cinch.*

Plan in detail

An excellent way to prevent future problems is to make plans specific and detailed. Although some details may change along the way, giving them forethought is always a good idea. When enthusiastic about a new pursuit, it's easy to take details for granted. It's a mistake to think "That part will be easy; I will figure it out when the time comes." A thorough plan doesn't take anything for granted. When planning the details, you may discover something you thought was going to be simple, quick, or cheap is not so after all. Like examining all of the small pieces of a motor, planning the details is a good way to keep your plan running smoothly.

> *It is said that victorious warriors win first, and then go to war. (Sun Tzu)*

> *It isn't the mountain ahead that wears you out; it's the pebble in your shoe. (Robert Service)*

Look for the obstacles

Making a list of possible obstacles and another list of possible solutions is a great way to fortify your plan. Remember: a chain is only as strong as its weakest link. Look for the weak links in your plan and then create ideas to strengthen them.

Be flexible

Make your plans as specific and detailed as you can, but also make them flexible. Unexpected obstacles and roadblocks can hinder your progress at times. They might bring your progress to a screeching halt. This is to be expected and prepared for. Spend time in the planning stage considering how you might make progress toward your main goal, but using some alternate methods and routes. In other words, have a plan B and maybe a plan C for reaching various milestones.

> *In military operations, formlessness is the most effective. Just as water has no constant shape, adapt as you face the enemy. (Sun Tzu)*

> *Better twice measured than once wrong. (Danish Proverb)*

> *Don't think there are no crocodiles because the water is calm. (Malayan proverb)*

The Importance of Networking

It's become cliché. We hear all the time that we need to constantly network; *that it's not what you know, it's who you know*. It's easy to understand this concept. Who wouldn't want to have a small (or large) army of contacts that could spread the word about our businesses for us? That would make life much easier. And we know there are many outlets and tools available to facilitate our networking efforts. Facebook, Twitter, LinkedIn, your local chamber of commerce, BNI, local business-card-exchange meetings, and other opportunities are always there for us to use. In theory, it seems so easy.

In reality, it's not so easy. It takes work—steady, continuous, and sometimes tedious work. There is no doubt, however, that your network of contacts is one of your greatest assets in business, if not your greatest asset. Cultivating your network of contacts might be the most beneficial investment of time you can spend for your business. Although it's not easy, it need not be that difficult, either. Once a few new tasks and habits become part of your routine, you are ready to reap the benefits of networking.

There are many great books on the subject of networking (my favorite is "Networking Like a Pro," by Ivan Misner and David Alexander). Much can be learned from those who do it well. Creating a strategy is a good start. Consider questions like: *What specific people would it be good to have a connection with? What types of people would be good additions to my network? Is there a particular way I would be most comfortable introducing myself?*

Networking Basic Principles

Networking really involves two basic steps: Meeting people, and keeping in touch with them. If you are doing those things, you are networking. Of course, there are many different ways that we might meet people. And there are many different ways we might keep in touch with them. There are more ways than ever now to do both of those things. Everyone needs to decide for themselves what methods are most appropriate and appealing for them.

Whatever one's methods for meeting people and keeping in touch are, there are helpful principles to keep in mind. These principles are timeless and will not change because of technology or anything else:

- There needs to be an authentic human connection. Although it may be a thin and loose connection, it needs to be there. Someone might accept a friend request on Facebook, but is that a real human connection? Not if they have never met you and don't know anything about you.

- Keeping in touch is considered the Golden Rule of networking. The phrase out of sight, out of mind applies in human relationships. If you don't make occasional contact with the people you know, they might forget the things you could do for them, or what they can do for you.

- It's best to have a "giving" attitude. Be mindful of ways in which you can help others. If your only motivation is to get something from them, people will be less interested in you and your offerings. A willingness to listen, appreciate, and help others goes a long way in your relationships.

- Be content to make slow, gradual progress. It's not a sprint, it's a marathon.

- Your network of contacts will work for you, even while you sleep. If you establish yourself as a friendly person that provides a useful service, referrals can be generated that bring you new business.

- Having a systematic approach for keeping in touch is important. Pick certain days and intervals for keeping in touch with people. Perhaps it's to make phone calls, write emails, or maybe write hand-written notes. Or perhaps you would like to use social web platforms to interact with people in your network. Taking the time to read their Facebook, Google+, or LinkedIn posts, and then commenting on them is a good way to keep in touch.

How to get started

To get started with networking, the best thing to do is consider all of the people you know in your life, such as your relatives, friends, coworkers, customers, etc. It's important to value those relationships. Ask yourself: Do you appreciate those people? Are you grateful for having them in your life? Are you willing to listen to them, help them occasionally, and keep in closer touch with them? The answers to those questions should be "yes" if you truly want to be a good networker.

Next, consider the methods you might use for keeping in touch with people. As I mentioned, having a systematic approach is best. Setting aside time on certain days of the week for contacting people is a good way to go. Perhaps you would send five "hello" emails every Thursday morning. Or perhaps you would use social websites daily like LinkedIn or Google Plus for twenty minutes after lunch. Choose a routine that will be easy to maintain, and that you will enjoy. Keeping it going over the long haul should be your main goal.

Next, consider ways to expand your network. There are many ways to meet new people. It's easy to underestimate how often we have the opportunity. We don't need to make chit-chat with every person with whom we are on an elevator, or seated next to on an airplane. But expanding your network requires an attitude of openness, candor and generosity. It's about authentic, human connections. Find a way to interact with people that you will enjoy, and will be mutually beneficial.

Some general networking tips

- Listen more than you talk.
- Don't be too serious.
- Don't be in a rush.
- Look for ways to be helpful.
- Be cheerful and upbeat.
- Don't brag.
- Make yourself known for one thing.
- Send thank-you notes, or "nice-to-meet-you" emails.
- Always, always follow up.
- Keep a record of who you meet, when you met them, and details from your conversation.

The Power of Optimism

To be a successful entrepreneur, optimism should be a driving force for progress. Working wholeheartedly toward a goal requires a firm belief that it can be achieved. We must believe in our plans, abilities, and fortitude. An optimistic attitude will give us further momentum when things are going well, and help us get through when things aren't going well. Optimism is a key ingredient in accomplishing difficult goals and succeeding in business.

Being optimistic doesn't mean you don't expect problems—it means believing you will overcome them. You will find a way to keep going forward. Optimists see problems not just as challenges, but as opportunities. Dealing with problems makes us better at what we do. There are good lessons in every problem we encounter. (Pessimists only see the negative side when problems arise. Rather than work to find the solution, they tend to give up quickly.)

> "A pessimist sees the difficulty in every opportunity; an optimist sees the opportunity in every difficulty." (Sir Winston Churchill)

Benefits of optimism

- Helps you work harder
- Helps you work better
- Helps you be more resilient
- Gives you less stress
- Has a contagious effect toward others
- Inspires confidence in others
- Helps you be more persistent
- Helps you learn the lessons that are available

Ways to be more optimistic

- Have an optimistic phrase that you repeat many times each day. (Muhammad Ali stayed optimistic by constantly uttering "I am the greatest… I am the greatest of all time.")
- Visualize progress and success. Keep mental pictures that are as detailed as possible
- Continuously reaffirm a tangible goal. (The actor Jim Carrey used to keep a check in his wallet made out to himself for one million dollars. He repeatedly said to himself and others "One day, I'm going to cash that check.")
- Use the words "I can" often, and avoid the words "I can't."
- Always look for the positive side of things.
- Don't complain, criticize or make excuses.
- Be inspired by true stories of people overcoming great odds.
- Give yourself a pat on the back sometimes.
- Smile more.
- Learn to manage or ignore the things you can't change.
- Find things to marvel at.

The story of the two shoe salesmen

Two shoe salesmen working for different manufacturers traveled to the same country in Africa, attempting to find a new market for selling shoes. The first salesman looked around at the people, then called the home office and said, "This is pointless… The people here don't even wear shoes… We will never sell any." The second salesman looked around at the people, then called the home office and said, "Send me everything! We can sell shoes to the whole country!"

The story of the optimist child and the pessimist child

A man had two sons. One was an extreme optimist and the other was an extreme pessimist. He decided to teach them both a lesson. He told them he had a surprise gift for each of them. To the pessimist child he gave a room full of beautiful toys. To the optimist child he gave a big pile of horse manure. When the pessimist child saw the room full of toys, he started crying. "What's wrong?" said the father. The son said "The toys are so beautiful that I'm afraid I will break them if I play with them." When the optimist child saw the pile of horse manure, he started laughing, jumping and celebrating. "Why are you so happy?" said the father. The son said "With all of this horse manure, there must be a pony around here somewhere!"

The Power of Persistence

This is another topic that has become cliché. There are books, articles, and slogans abundant that promote the virtues of persistence. It's easy to understand this concept, but it's difficult to apply in reality. Why is it so difficult to be persistent? Because trying to accomplish goals is often very frustrating. There are challenges along the way—some are expected, some unexpected. It takes great determination to keep pushing forward. The people around us are often no help. Rather than encouraging you to keep going, they suggest you raise the white flag, saying "It will never work"… "Better luck next time" …or "Well, at least you tried."

Great things are accomplished through great determination. Great determination is a rare thing. We don't see it very often in others or in ourselves. This is why people tend to give up easily on their goals and dreams, and expect others around them to do the same. It's true, obviously, that not everything is possible. I doubt anyone will ever successfully build a time-travel machine or a tree that grows neckties. Then again, who ever thought man would be able to fly to the moon or talk long-distance across the globe? Amazing things can happen if we are determined and persistent. If we keep looking, we can find ways to get around the obstacles that impede us. There is a saying that "fortune favors the bold." It is true that through bold determination and persistence we can often break through and find a way to keep going.

The story of Thomas Edison's light bulb is a great story of persistence. For decades, scientists knew how to create artificial light with electricity. The problem was that it only lasted a few seconds. It would never be practical to use until someone figured out a way to make the illumination last much longer. Thomas Edison was determined to find the solution to that problem. His experiments led to failure upon failure upon failure. But he kept going. He believed that there was a way, and that he would find it. Eventually he discovered that if a vacuum was created within a glass bulb, the filament could stay lit for long periods of time. This discovery was of massive significance, and gave the world the use of electrical lighting. Again, great accomplishments are the result of great determination and persistence.

There are innumerable stories of success in business that are based on steady, stubborn, and relentless persistence. Some of the people who have become legendary figures were thought to be foolish and irrational by the people around them. But they kept going. A good friend of mine often says, "You need to be like a dog with a sock in its mouth… bite hard and don't give it up."

> *Nothing in the world can take the place of persistence. Talent will not; nothing is more common than unsuccessful men with talent. Genius will not; unrewarded genius is almost a proverb. Education will not; the world is full of educated failures. Persistence and determination alone are omnipotent. (Calvin Coolidge)*
>
> *The reasonable man adapts himself to the world. The unreasonable one persists in trying to adapt the world to himself. Therefore, all progress depends on the unreasonable man. (George Bernard Shaw)*

The Power of Focus

An interviewer once asked Bill Gates and Warren Buffet what the greatest key to their success was. They both gave the same one-word answer: focus. This is another concept that is easy to understand but difficult to put into practice. There is so much going on around us with our friends, family, hobbies, work, etc., that it's easy to get distracted and scattered. Also, there is so much opportunity around us. It takes austere discipline and "tunnel-vision" to stay focused on a single major goal.

My favorite quote about the importance of focus comes from the legendary showman P.T. Barnum. This is what he says (I underlined my favorite part):

Do not scatter your powers. Engage in one kind of business only, and stick to it faithfully until you succeed or until you conclude to abandon it. <u>A constant hammering on one nail will generally drive it home at last, so that it can be clinched.</u> When a man's undivided attention is centered on one object, his mind will constantly be suggesting improvements of value which would escape him if his brain were occupied by a dozen different subjects at once.

The metaphor of "a constant hammering on one nail" resonates with me. Think about the power and energy of a hammer hitting a nail. What if that energy were spread wider and wider? It wouldn't yield nearly as much power. If you have a specific goal, and all of your power and energy is focused on it, you will have the best chance of success.

One of the most difficult aspects of concentrating our energy is that it requires elimination. It requires a boldness that many of us don't possess. There is a risk involved in putting all of our energy toward one main goal. What if it doesn't work out? What if your time, energy, and resources end up being wasted? It takes courage to eliminate certain distractions, activities, and other goals from our lives. But that courage is what it takes to achieve a difficult goal. Ask yourself if you have a clear and specific primary goal, and if you are willing to eliminate other goals, activities, and distractions in order to achieve it.

Here are some helpful tips for staying highly focused:

- Start your day by accomplishing the most important tasks for your goal.
- Be disciplined about the time you spend on email, phone calls, social websites, reading the news, and other distractions that can pull your time and energy.
- Have a systematic way of getting things done, and be very strict about it.
- Avoid multitasking.

- Be as specific as possible about your goal and the milestones to reach it.

- Be sure to make progress every single day.

- Avoid conflicts.

- Keep a reminder of your main goal in a place where you will see it every day. (A good example of this is from the late-singer Michael Jackson. While recording one of his albums, he put a note on his mirror that said "100 million." His goal was to sell 100 million copies of his new album. He didn't end up selling that many, but he did sell a lot!)

One does not accumulate, but eliminate. It is not daily increase but daily decrease. The height of cultivation always runs to simplicity. (Bruce Lee)

The Power of Habit

Do we control our habits? Or do our habits control us? To say that the power of habit is immense would be an understatement. Habits serve as the basis for most of the things we do. There are many things we do every day without much consideration because they are habits. We do things a certain way because that's the way we've always done them. Habits can give a comforting structure to our lives. They are like guideposts. But are they guiding us in the direction we want to go?

To be successful and live the life you want, it's important to be a master of your habits (instead of the other way around). The first step toward controlling your habits is simply believing that you can. If you don't believe you can, then you really can't. If you do believe you can, then you really can. Even *that* is a habit! If you struggle with believing you can control your habits, you need to focus on changing that self-defeating attitude.

If you believe that you can control your habits, then you can control the direction of your life. It's important to pay attention, and be aware of your habits. P.T. Barnum wrote that "money is like fire; a wonderful servant, but a terrible master." I suppose that habits can be one or the other as well. Consider ways you could change your habits to become more productive. At the beginning of this section, I wrote about time management. Time management is a great thing to consider when trying to adopt better habits. Do you spend too much time checking emails, reading news stories, or looking at Facebook? Evaluate the habits you could change to become more productive.

Habitual Thinking

Just as we are creatures of habit in our actions, so we are in our thoughts. It's a fact that the more we hear and think the same ideas, the more we adjust to them and believe them. Habitual thinking is an immense force in defining who we are. From the time we are infants we begin absorbing information and certain outlooks on the world. Our parents, experiences, and other influences instill thoughts into our young, malleable brains with frequent repetition. By the time we are five years old, we have an interpretation of reality that has been shaped by hundreds of thousands of influences. If you want to become more focused, optimistic, and productive, consider trying to change habitual thought patterns that might be holding you back. They key is: repetition.

> *Like a wheel, inside a wheel, inside of you…. what you believe about yourself all comes true. (John Mellencamp)*

Ways to help control your habits

- Start with small steps.
- Several times per day, visualize a new habit taking hold.
- If you have a bad habit, find a substitute for it.
- Stay away from temptations.
- Be more aware of your habits.
- Make it a game for which you get points and bonuses.

Ten Things Every Entrepreneur Should Know

Your beliefs become your thoughts,
Your thoughts become your words,
Your words become your actions,
Your actions become your habits,
Your habits become your values,
Your values become your destiny. (Aristotle)

Summary

- Managing time is one of our greatest challenges. Prioritizing your goals is the most important aspect of time management. A lack of time is a lack of priorities.

- Our network of contacts is one of our greatest assets. To grow your network, it helps to take a genuine interest in people and have a giving attitude. Keeping in touch is a must.

- One of the most important things for an entrepreneur to know is how to be a good planner. For big goals, it helps to plan in stages, plan in detail, and incorporate as much flexibility as possible.

- Reputation is one of the most significant assets in business. It takes many years to build a good reputation, but almost no time for it to be destroyed. It should be fiercely protected.

- Social proof is a psychological phenomenon that influences people to follow the lead of others. Social proof can positively affect your reputation, and your reputation can positively affect your social proof. Elements of social proof can be very effective in marketing.

- Referrals can be the lifeblood of your business. Happy customers are often willing to give referrals. It's important to ask for them systematically. Having a regular habit of asking for referrals can lead to substantial growth for your business.

- Great successes are usually the result of great partnerships. It's important to be open to partnerships, but not to rush into them. Choosing the right people or businesses to partner with is a big decision.

- To be a successful entrepreneur, optimism should be a driving force behind you. To work relentlessly and wholeheartedly, you must hold a belief that you will overcome any obstacles that impede you. Remember that every obstacle holds lessons and opportunities that can make you stronger.

- Persistence is perhaps the most important quality for success. It takes a stubborn and relentless determination to keep going in the face of great obstacles. Some of the most successful and legendary figures were thought to be foolish and irrational by the people around them—but they kept going.

- Bill Gates and Warren Buffet both consider focus to be the greatest key to their success. It's difficult to remain highly focused. It takes austere discipline to ignore and eliminate distractions. Your energy and power should be focused like a hammer hitting a nail.

- Habits serve as the basis for most things that we do. The more we can control them, the more we can affect the direction of our lives. Not only do habits affect our actions, but they affect our way of thinking. If you can change your habitual thoughts, you have a much greater power over your destiny.

Part 10−Putting Your Plan into Action (Realistically)

In Parts 1-9, I tried to give you a fairly objective description of the methods, tools, services, and principles that can help your Internet marketing efforts succeed. I also included some of my recommendations along the way. My hope is that you now have a better overall understanding of what your options are. Some of the methods I've written about are easy to implement. Others are more difficult and require long-term commitments in order to reap the benefits. You need to carefully consider which methods will be beneficial for your type of business, and the amount of time and money you're willing to invest in them. As I mentioned in the introduction, it's easy to get overwhelmed. Trying to do too much is a mistake. Not setting clear priorities is also a mistake. If you're like me, you get overly eager sometimes trying to seize every opportunity. It's not possible to seize every opportunity; there are too many opportunities available. Do yourself a favor and take a realistic approach that has clear priorities.

In Part 10, I am going to recap information from other sections of this book in a prioritized fashion. I'm putting the information into two categories: Must-Do and Must-Consider. The Must-Do items are the ones I strongly recommend, because of their high ROI (return-on-investment) potential. They are the most important things to do to keep your business "in the game" of Internet marketing. I recommend using the Must-Do items as a checklist, but again, you must consider the ones that make the most sense for your type of business and prioritize for yourself. By all means, rearrange the list as you see fit. Omit items if you want to forgo those methods, or add others that aren't mentioned in this book. I hope my list will be a good starting point for your own realistic game plan.

In the introduction of this book, I wrote, "*How are we supposed to do all of those things? How are we even supposed to learn all of those things?*" You might be thinking this as you read my Must-Do items below. I would like you to make steady progress, not be overwhelmed. Refer to your own priority list, and go at your own pace. Also, keep focused on the main target for each of these Must-Do items. Be sure to review the sections of this book where I list key point summaries, such as "The most important things to know," "The most important things to do," and "The most important things NOT to do."

Must-Do

Make your website a top priority

> For most businesses, the website is of key importance. It's how you present yourself to the world. It is the "tip of the spear" for all of your Internet marketing efforts. Ultimately, you want all of your other channels (Facebook, YouTube, etc.) to bring traffic to your website. Your website should have information that is well presented and useful. It should make visitors feel comfortable. It should have a look and feel that says "this is a credible business, run by real people."

Make sure your website has these qualities

Here are some important qualities of an effective website:

- Easy navigation
- A clear CTA (call-to-action)
- Appealing images, especially of human faces
- Consistent color and style elements
- Fast-loading pages
- Content that looks fresh and updated
- An effort to say "We want to serve your needs," rather than "We want to tell you how wonderful we are."

Make sure your website doesn't suffer from these ailments

Here are the things to avoid (some of which correlate with the previous list):

- Overloaded web pages that look cluttered and unfocused

- Cold-looking pages, lacking a human touch
- Inconsistent color and style elements
- Confusing navigation
- A lack of fresh and current-looking content
- Having pages that load slowly
- Misspellings and bad grammar
- Making the site about you instead of about your customers

Do on-page SEO

On-page SEO refers to adding keywords to your web pages so that they will be indexed correctly by the search engines (SEO stands for "search engine optimization"). When search engine spiders crawl web pages, they look at different things to get an indication of the subject material. One of the key things they look at is the "title." The title appears at the very top of the browser window or tab when a page is loaded. It is put in the "header" section of the html code, which holds information that is not part of the page content itself. Other important on-page SEO elements include meta-description tags, headings, text on your pages, and alt tags, which are words shown in place of images (for situations when the images don't load in a browser).

Consider your most important keywords carefully

Keyword research should not be taken lightly or rushed. Honing in on the best keywords for your business is one of the most important aspects of Internet marketing. Remember, you will be in competition with other businesses that might be using the same keywords as you. Can you set yourself apart by adding a longer tail? Adding a longer tail means adding words to narrow down the meaning. Here is an example of how a longer tail can be added:

- roses
- red roses
- long-stemmed red roses

- long-stemmed red roses in bulk

Also, do some research on Google's Keyword Planner tool. It will give you valuable information, such as ideas for keywords related to your business, as well as the number of times people have searched those keywords on Google in the previous year. (You must open an AdWords account to use this tool, but there will be no cost if you don't run any AdWords campaigns.)

Have a blog

I was reluctant to put blogging in the Must-Do category because it takes an investment of time on a regular basis that many people will find difficult to manage. However, the benefits of a blog are numerous. If you are serious about increasing your visibility online, having a blog really is a must-do thing. It keeps your website fresh with new content, which helps keep visitors looking at your site longer. It helps with search-engine-optimization, which will give you more traffic. It gives you something to promote through social websites, such as on your Facebook page (whenever you make a new blog post, you can offer the link to your fans and followers). Having a blog is the basis of a good content-marketing strategy. Having good content leads to high visibility on the Internet.

Register your local business with the search engines

The major search engines each have a special system for listing local businesses. The first step for local business owners to take is to register their business. This involves filling out an online form, and then going through a verification process. (They want to verify the accuracy of the address entered, so they send a postcard with a code to that address.) If you are a local business, showing up in these listings can be extremely valuable—at no cost to you.

Build citations for your business

Citations are mentions of your business on the web. Any mention of your business (especially if it includes the name, address, and phone number) is considered a citation. Citations help create

Putting Your Plan into Action (Realistically)

visibility for your business, bring traffic to your website, and lead to higher rankings in the local search results. You can easily build citations on directory sites like www.yellowbook.com. There are many directory sites that allow you to list your business without a cost. For a list of sites where you can build citations, go to www.brickway.net/building-citations/.

Keep a consistent NAP with all online citations

Anytime your business is mentioned or advertised online, make sure you use the same NAP (name, address and phone number). The search engines have an algorithmic approach for the ranking order in which local businesses appear in search results. Having multiple citations with a consistent NAP can positively influence a business' ranking. This gives the appearance of a more established and credible business. Any inconsistencies with the name, address, or phone number can cause your business to drop in ranking.

Create a Facebook business page

Facebook has roughly a billion users. Since so many people use Facebook, it is a mistake not to take advantage of this free page your business can have. People who visit your page and click the "like" button will then receive the posts from your business page in their news feeds. Your Facebook page can have a great deal of marketing value, without any cost to you. The important things to do are: create the page, add some images and information, and occasionally (at least) post new information related to your business. Also, be sure to interact with people who make comments on your posts.

Create a Google+ page

A business page on Google+ is similar to a business page on Facebook. Google+ doesn't get the same amount of traffic as Facebook, but it represents another opportunity to connect with people at no cost to you. Anyone who visits your page, and clicks the "+1" button, will receive your posts. Also, engaging with people through your Google+ page can help with your rankings in Google search results. (Facebook and Google+ business pages are also good citations to have!)

Use YouTube

YouTube is a massively popular website that allows you to upload videos for free. The videos can bring visibility to your business, and traffic to your website. "How-to" videos are extremely popular. One advantage to YouTube is that it doesn't demand the continuous engagement necessary for Twitter, Facebook, or Google+. With YouTube, you may simply create a video, upload it, tag it with keywords, and let it go to work for you. Your YouTube videos can show up whenever anyone searches YouTube or Google for the keywords used in your tags. Also, you could embed the videos in web pages on your site, or share the videos on Facebook, Google+ or other places.

Use email marketing

Email marketing is a must-do because it can be a fantastic marketing vehicle for very little time invested. The easiest way to approach it is to use an email marketing service. These services provide all you need to make your campaigns run smoothly. Giving away a free gift (such as a PDF file with information) can be a good incentive for people to submit their email address. Be aware that it's not okay to send emails to people who have not voluntarily submitted their email addresses. Spamming is not effective, and can get you into legal trouble. (For information on email marketing services, go to www.brickway.net/email-marketing-services/.)

Use Google AdWords

I don't know what type of business you're in, but there is a great possibility that AdWords can help grow your business quickly. It is a very powerful and flexible platform that gives you a high degree of control over the visibility and costs of advertising. AdWords is a PPC (pay-per-click) platform. With PPC, you have two simultaneous goals: to be visible to likely prospects, and invisible to everyone else. There is a steep learning curve to AdWords, so I strongly advise that you either study intensely or get some help. I am a certified AdWords specialist and would be glad to help (www.brickway.net/contact/), or you can find others through Elance (www.elance.com).

Use Google Webmaster Tools

Google Webmaster Tools is a service meant to inform you of things related to your website from the Google search engine perspective. It's a free service, and it's easy to use. If you care about how your website is seen by the Google search engine, you should take advantage of Google Webmaster Tools. It can give you such information as: errors that might have occurred when the Googlebot crawled your site; traffic data about how people arrived at your site; keyword data that tells what keywords are seen as most prominent; and search query data showing the actual queries made which resulted in an appearance of one of your pages in search results. It does not take much of your time. Just sign up for an account and add your website. Then look occasionally at the information it offers.

Use Google Analytics

Google Analytics is another service offered by Google to give insight on how your website is performing. Although there are some similarities to Google Webmaster Tools, the two services have different purposes. Google Webmaster Tools is meant to give you information related to how the Googlebot sees your site, and certain data points regarding your site's appearances in the Google search results. Google Analytics is a much bigger and more robust platform for analyzing your web traffic from all sources, not just the Google search engine. Google Analytics is the best tool for gauging the success of marketing efforts to drive traffic to your website, and for learning visitor actions when they arrive. It will tell you how many visitors each page on your site receives, the average amount of time visitors spend on your pages, the type of device they are using, and much more. Google Analytics can be linked to a Google Webmaster Tools account, and also to a Google AdWords account. Using Google Analytics is a must-do if you are serious about Internet marketing. It's free to use, easy to check, and offers valuable data to help guide your marketing efforts and investments.

Others must-do points from this book

Humanize. People like to do business with people, not computers. Adding images, stories, interactive features, humor, and other human touches can go a long way to make your Internet presence more appealing.

Make specific goals. Making your goals as specific as possible makes them easier to accomplish. Consider the goals you have at the moment and how you could make them as specific and concrete as possible.

Plan in detail. A former general spoke about the three most important parts of military planning: logistics, logistics, and logistics. It's one thing to get heavy equipment into the right battle positions. It's another thing to ensure that they always have enough fuel, ammunition, extra parts, etc. The more detailed you make your plans, the more you are able to foresee difficulties and prepare for them.

Be stern about time-management. Time-management is one of the biggest challenges in business. To manage your time in the best way, be sure to have clear priorities and be willing to eliminate distractions and goals of lesser importance. Also, be sure you are using the best tools for organization and communication.

Be optimistic. An optimistic attitude is a key ingredient for success. It's what helps us keep going through the most difficult days, and makes us more effective on our better days.

Use social proof when you can. Social proof refers to the tendency of people to believe that others know more about a situation, and that we should follow their lead. Social proof influences our decisions at many points in our life. Ways to use this in your favor are to include testimonials on your website, show continuous interaction with people on your Facebook page, or highlighting statistics (like McDonalds: *"billions and billions served"*).

Discover your USP. A USP (*unique selling proposition*) sets you apart from your competition. It highlights some advantage your products or services has over ones from the competition. Simply put, it gives a reason why customers should do business with you.

Sell the benefits. Selling the benefits means explaining how your products or services will be helpful to prospective customers. Most businesses make the mistake of selling the features instead. For example, a feature of a vacuum cleaner might be: stronger suction. The benefit is that you can vacuum better and faster, saving time and creating a cleaner environment.

Use images. Images are perhaps your most effective tool in marketing. When you see television commercials or magazine ads, notice how powerful they are. They can communicate messages, convey emotions, or tell stories. They may also give a glimpse into how life could be better with your product of service. When it comes to the social web, images posts are looked at, commented on, and shared more than twice as much as text posts.

Tell stories. Facts tell, stories sell. People like stories. We are naturally curious about things that happen. By telling a story, you can hold a prospective customer's attention longer. Also, stories are easier to remember than straight facts. Incorporate storytelling as much as you can on your website and in your marketing.

Must-Consider

Try to get backlinks

Links to your website from other websites are called "backlinks." For many years, backlinks have been considered (by Google) to be a telling indicator of how valuable a web page is for content. If the Googlebot finds many links pointed to a certain page, an assumption is made that there must be good content on that page. This can cause a page to rank higher in the search results. The problem, however, is that a whole cottage industry has grown out of the demand for links in order to influence rankings. Google caught onto this, and has modified their algorithm as a result. Backlinks are still important for rankings, but only if they come from credible sites—especially ones that are about a similar topic. There are many ways to go about trying to get backlinks, including: writing guest posts on other people's blogs, asking for links from people in other businesses, and submitting press releases. If you are serious about SEO, spend some time trying to get quality backlinks.

Use Twitter

Twitter is an immensely popular social web platform. Using it is very simple: open a free account, and start posting messages (of 140 characters or less). Who will receive those messages? Other Twitter users who decide to follow you. Succeeding on Twitter has to do with both quantity and quality of tweets. To truly leverage this platform, it is advisable to tweet every day, preferably several times. The quality is very important as well. If you tweet a message that is particularly informative, interesting or funny, your followers may decide to RT (re-tweet) it to their followers. Everyone who gets the tweet can then decide to RT, making Twitter an extremely viral platform. Sharing interesting images and links is an effective tactic. The most important thing to remember is that it's a long-term, slow-building process. Make sure you are willing to keep the tweets flowing for a period of years.

Use LinkedIn

LinkedIn is the place where business owners, tradesmen, and professionals connect with one another. It is very popular, and can do wonders for a career or a business. Like other social web platforms, it requires continuous participation and engagement. It's not a set-and-forget type of thing. Laying the foundation for a good LinkedIn presence starts with creating your profile. Your profile is like an online resume: it's how other members will see you, and decide if they want to connect with you. A lot of business gets done through connections on LinkedIn. Features like recommendations and endorsements can help you build credibility. You can also create a company page, which other members can choose to follow. LinkedIn is free, but has a premium membership option that allows more features and freedoms.

Putting Your Plan into Action (Realistically)

Manage your online reviews

Reviews for businesses on websites like Yelp, Google and Yahoo are becoming more and more important to pay attention to. As the public usage of these services increases, businesses with high ratings and positive reviews are going to have a distinct advantage. The time is now to start paying attention to, and managing your reviews. Fortunately, there are some great tools available to help you monitor your reputation online. Some of which are also intended to help you cultivate good reviews from your happy customers. (I wrote about this in Part 9, in "The Importance of Reputation" section.)

Do podcasting

Podcasting means to record segments of audio and/or video, and make them available via RSS (Really Simple Syndication). It's a bit like blogging: if people like the podcast, they can subscribe to it. Your podcasts can be listed in iTunes and on other podcast directories. Podcasting is a great way to share your knowledge, and establish yourself as an expert. It is also a great medium for interviews. Podcasting has been known to be a huge boon for some businesses. The demand by the public seems to be getting greater for podcast content, fueled by the growing usage of smartphones. There are several services available that make the process of podcasting smooth and easy.

Use Craigslist

Craigslist is one of the most popular websites in the world, receiving roughly fifty billion page views per month. Craigslist is mostly used for classified advertising in local markets. It allows you to post to one category, in one city, every 48 hours. For most types of ads (and in most locations), there is no charge for advertising on Craigslist. If your business provides a service, you may post an ad under the "services offered" category. Visitors to Craigslist are able to browse ads, or do keyword searches to find what they are seeking. Since Craigslist receives such a large amount of traffic, it's worthwhile to experiment to see if Craigslist might be helpful to your business.

Have a mobile-friendly website

A mobile website is a version of your website that's easier to read and use on a smartphone. This is an important thing to consider because people are using their smartphones more and more for web activity. Providing web pages that are mobile-friendly makes it easier for the people using those devices to find what they are looking for. Large, easy-to-press buttons can say "Call Now," "Directions," or other messages. Pressing a "Call Now" button can initiate a phone call. Since mobile-browsing has become a new norm, keep your website as mobile-friendly as possible.

Use a CMS, like WordPress

A CMS (content management system) allows you to have a well-structured and attractive website, without having to know programming code. Through a back-end interface, a CMS lets you create pages and posts. You can add text, photos, videos, links, menus and other items to your pages and posts. When new pages or posts are completed, you can publish them to be seen on the front-end. The most popular CMS is called WordPress. WordPress is widely recognized as the easiest to use among the most popular CMS platforms. It has a huge number of themes and plug-ins available, it's free to use, and it provides great resources for learning.

Other must-consider points from this book

Use Evernote. Evernote is a software program for organizing your notes. Rather than have information spread out in different places, you may use Evernote as your personal database of information. It's very easy to input new information, as well as to access it later. Also, your data gets synchronized to all of your devices. It is free to use, but also has a premium version. Organization is a key aspect of work efficiency and time management. I believe Evernote is the most useful tool for staying organized.

Use Gmail. Gmail is the email platform owned by Google. It is far more useful, though, than just an email platform. Its powerful search function makes it useful as a database system itself. It allows you to manage other email accounts from within, and filter messages to keep your mail sorted and organized automatically. For example, you can set emails from a certain source to be automatically deleted, automatically forwarded, or automatically labeled and archived.

Use Elance. Elance is a service that provides a connection to skilled professional freelancers around the world. When you need a graphic designer, email marketing specialist, or someone to design an iPhone app for your business, you can post the job on the Elance website and receive bids from around the world. Elance has a very easy and reliable interface. Finding freelancers through Elance can be an enormous time (and money) saver for your business. There is no cost for using the Elance service to post jobs. When a freelancer is hired, funds go into an escrow account. They are released to the freelancer when the job is completely satisfactorily.

Use Hootsuite. If you plan on using several social websites, I highly recommend using Hootsuite. It is a tool that allows you to manage several different social web accounts and pages from a single interface. It's loaded with features that can make your social web efforts more effective and less time-consuming. It's free to use, but has a premium version.

Always be testing. Testing should always be part of your process with Internet marketing. In fact, it's one of the most significant things you can do to improve. When you test, you learn things that you would not be able to know or predict otherwise. Whenever you can, try to make A/B testing part of your process. For example, use AdWords to rotate and test two different promotions or discounts to see which gets a better response. If you do email marketing, try sending the same message to the whole list, but with a different subject-line to half of it. Then you can learn which has greater appeal.

Must-NOT-Do

- Underestimate the importance of having an effective website
- Underestimate the importance of having a blog

- Underestimate the time and discipline required to maintain a blog and a social web presence
- Ignore the power of mobile (people are using their smartphones more and more to access the web)
- Ignore the power and flexibility of AdWords
- Ignore the power of images to communicate messages and convey emotions
- Ignore the power of stories to grab people's attention and create more memorable messages
- Ignore the importance of setting clear priorities and specific goals
- Ignore the power of social proof
- Forget to register your local business with the search engines
- Forget to build citations for your business on directory sites (especially if you have a local business)
- Forget to do basic on-page SEO for all web pages you would like to show in search results
- Forget the importance of reputation
- Forget to systematically ask for referrals
- Try to be something or someone you are not
- Try to do too much at once (be content with steady progress)
- Lack a human touch (use humor, stories, and images to warm up your pages and posts)
- Have an inconsistent NAP (name, address, phone number) for your business on the web
- Spend money on AdWords/PPC without knowing what you are doing, or without getting qualified help
- Confuse "search" PPC advertising with "display" PPC advertising (AdWords lets you do either or both)

Putting Your Plan into Action (Realistically)

- Rush the process of choosing your most important keywords (especially for SEO)
- Promote features instead of benefits
- Make your marketing all about you, instead of about your customer's needs
- Assume you know what prospective customers care about (it's better to listen to them first)
- Scatter your energy on too many things (as P.T. Barnum wrote, concentrate your energy "like a hammer on a nail.")
- Procrastinate

In Closing

Writing this book was fun for me. I hope reading it was helpful to you. I'll end with this riddle:

Five frogs were sitting on a log at the edge of a pond. Four of the frogs decided to jump into the pond. How many frogs were left sitting on the log? Answer: Five. Deciding to jump in and actually jumping in are two different things.

(Follow me on Twitter: @brickwaybarry)

Appendix

Here is a list of links that appear in this book (in order of appearance):

Contact Me
www.brickway.net/contact/

Supplements to this book
www.brickway.net/strategybook/supplements/

Tools for speed-testing your website
www.brickway.net/strategybook/page-load-speed/

Web hosting service
www.brickway.net/bluehost/

Domain name registration service
www.brickway.net/bluehost-domain-names/

Popular CMS platforms
www.wordpress.org
www.joomla.org
www.drupal.org

SmallBiz WordPress Theme
www.brickway.net/smallbiztheme/

Places to look for WordPress themes
www.themeforest.com
www.eleganthemes.com
www.ithemes.com

To start learning WordPress
www.wordpress.org

Google Webmaster Tools
www.google.com/webmasters/tools/

Bing Webmaster Tools
www.bing.com/toolbox/webmaster/

Google Analytics
www.google.com/analytics/

Install Google Analytics tracking code on your WordPress website
www.brickway.net/install-analytics-tracking-code-in-wordpress/

Directory sites for building citations
www.dexknows.com
www.yellowbook.com
www.merchantcircle.com
www.yelp.com
www.yellowpages.com
www.supermedia.com
www.manta.com
www.local.com
www.citysearch.com
www.patch.com

More extensive list of directory sites for building citations
www.brickway.net/building-citations/

Register your local business with the major search engines
www.google.com/+/business/
www.listings.local.yahoo.com/
www.bingplaces.com/

Services to create your mobile website
www.brickway.net/mobile-website-service/

Bing's Platform for PPC
www.bingads.microsoft.com

Facebook Advertising
www.facebook.com/ads/

Twitter Advertising
www.ads.twitter.com

LinkedIn Advertising
www.linkedin.com/advertising/

Keyword tools
Use Google's Keyword Planner within an AdWords account www.adwords.google.com
www.bing.com/toolbox/keywords/ (must sign up for a Bing Webmaster Tools account)
www.wordtracker.com
www.ubersuggest.org

SEO Tools
www.tools.seobook.com
www.hubspot.com
www.raventools.com
www.majesticseo.com
www.opensiteexplorer.org

Facebook for Business
www.facebook.com

Twitter for Business
www.twitter.com

LinkedIn
www.linkedin.com

Google+ for Business
www.plus.google.com

YouTube
www.youtube.com

Email marketing services
www.brickway.net/email-marketing-services/

CAN-SPAM Act of 2003
www.brickway.net/can-spam-act/

Podcasting services
www.spreaker.com
www.buzzsprout.com
www.podbean.com
www.blogtalkradio.com

www.mixlr.com

Craigslist
www.craigslist.com

Other classified ad sites
www.usfreeads.com
www.backpage.com
www.yahoo.classifieds.com
www.ezilonclassifiedads.com
www.highlandclassifieds.com

Evernote
www.evernote.com

Gmail
www.gmail.com

Elance
www.elance.com

Hootsuite
www.hootsuite.com

Jing
www.techsmith.com/download/jing/

IFTTT
www.ifttt.com

Dropbox
www.dropbox.com

Remember The Milk
www.rememberthemilk.com

Google Keyword Planner
www.adwords.google.com (You must have an AdWords account to use the Keyword Planner Tool.)

LastPass
www.lastpass.com

Finding creative commons photos on Flickr
www.flickr.com/creativecommons/.

Stock image services
www.dreamstime.com/
www.shutterstock.com/
www.istockphoto.com/
www.jupiterimages.com/
www.punchstock.com/
www.acclaimimages.com/
www.alamy.com/

Testing services
www.brickway.net/tools-for-testing/

Reputation monitoring services
www.getfivestars.com
www.google.com/alerts/
www.alerts.yahoo.com
www.twitter.com/search-home/
www.socialmention.com
www.trackur.com

Thanks

I would like to thank a few people who were helpful and supportive while I wrote this book. They taught me important things, gave me encouragement, gave me feedback, and even rescued my laptop from a TSA checkpoint at the Seattle-Tacoma airport. They are:

- Karla Abraham
- Rosie Abraham
- Joby Saad
- Brian Joseph
- Eileen Lonergan
- Don Campbell
- Thomas Hasch
- Rod Long
- Marc Chestnut

www.ingramcontent.com/pod-product-compliance
Lightning Source LLC
Chambersburg PA
CBHW051649170526
45167CB00001B/396